Cogito, Ergo Philosophus

« JE PENSE, DONC JE PHILOSOPHE »

I THINK, THEREFORE I PHILOSOPHIZE

THE CHRONICLES OF A SURVIVALIST

BEN WOOD JOHNSON

V̈

TESKO PUBLISHING

TESKO PUBLISHING
Middletown, Pennsylvania

Published and printed in the United States of America by Tesko Publishing
(Independent Press)

Paperback format

ISBN-13: 978-1-948600-06-4 (paperback)
ISBN-10: 1-948600-06-4 (paperback

Cover images

Copyright holder not raced. Any copyright concerned should be directed to the address
listed above. If contacted by the copyright holder, the publisher would make the
necessary adjustments and provide proper credits in subsequent reprints. Cover
illustration by Wood Oliver. For more information about the author, visit his website at
www.drbenwoodjohnson.com

Typeset in Garamond

In memory of my grandfather Fritz (Papa Fritz)
He was the thinker the world never thought about

ACKNOWLEDGMENT

THIS BOOK CAME ABOUT because of several individuals whom are dear to my heart. When I shared my understandings about the nature of human *Beingness* in the world, they encouraged me to examine the topic at length. This work is also inspired by the infinite struggles of my compatriots from the Republic of Haiti. They are the survivors of the world. They gave me the inspiration to explore the notion of *human existence* from a pragmatic lens.

TABLE OF CONTENTS

Table of Contents

PREFACE

THERE IS A LINK BETWEEN human thinking and human survival. As a way to explain that correlation as convincingly as possible, I proclaim *Cogito, Ergo Philosophus*, which means, I think, therefore I philosophize. I will elaborate on this notion further as I develop my arguments.

As a living being, I am always in charge of my *Beingness*; at least I think I am. Over and above, however, I could not make the irreconcilable argument that I am free to be however I want and whenever I want. I must recognize the limits of my *Beingness*.

I could not say that I am free to be as I see fit. I could not be free to be no matter how I would like to be. I could not be free to be no matter why I want to be. I could not be free to be no matter when I would like to be. Thus, I *could be* whenever *I could only be*.

While I might be *free to be*, I could only be *free to be* to the extent of my *Beingness*. I could only be depending of my inherent disposition to be. Based on that understanding, it could be said that I enjoy little or no immediate control over my being other than what my *Beingness* allows.

My biggest challenge in the world is to locate my *Beingness*. Except that, accomplishing this task is not always possible. In spite of my reality, I have to find the means to prolong my *Beingness*.

My point is that regardless of my personal hurdles, I have to survive beyond serendipity. I *have to be,* even if the conditions might not be propitious for me *to be* beyond chance. Barring other circumstances, what might hamper my *Beingness*? A barrier to consider is society. Another major obstacle is *Mother Nature*.

The being is bound in nature. Outside of the natural, there are no other ways for the being *to be*. Still, the being must improvise. He must find a way to be. He must do so beyond chance. The problem is that the being often falls short of meeting this goal.

In this work, I propose to examine the nature of human *Beingness*. I reckon this is a daunting task. But there is a big gap in the literature.

For many centuries, thinkers and philosophers alike have sought to explain the nature of human ontology. Few works have provided satisfactory answers to some of the most burning questions human beings have asked themselves. This work will probably not bridge this analytical gap.

Before we delve deeper in our discussion, let me note that I could not compile the manuscript the way I originally intended. The subject is very complex. The ideas echoed here are featured in two other works, which are complementary to the present text. They consist of the books titled *We Have No Clue* and *Owners of the World*.

The present installment contains eleven chapter and three sections. They comprise the following: (1) The nature of a thought; (2) Characteristics of a thought; and (3) Thinking and human domination.

The text includes an introductory section, which sets the stage for the arguments echoed in the document. That section introduces the subject, though not in length. The final section includes an index, the sources cited, my notes, and a segment about the author.

This compilation is based on a series of essays about human existence. The hope is to provide valuable insights on some of the most salient questions, which are often echoed in the literature. But the primary focus here is human survival.

I hope this work will contribute to the current discourse on the subject. I hope it will become a valuable addition to the literature. If not, I hope it will become a reference in your personal library.

This work offers is a candid narration about the human story. But be mindful this is a story told from a narrow perspective. In any case, I hope this book will engage your intellectual curiosity. I hope it will incite you to learn more about the subject.

It took me a while to come up with the right tone to convey my arguments. It took me a while to find a way to harmonize my thoughts. In any case, I had much fun compiling this book. I hope you will have a similar experience reading it.

Before we go farther in the debate, let me clarify what I mean by the *Cogito*. Let me reveal my most intimate idiosyncrasies about the subject. Without further delay, let us get to it...

Ben Wood Johnson, Ph.D.
February 19, 2019
Pennsylvania/USA
Updated 03/2020

INTRODUCTION

"What I have to say is not what they want to hear. I will speak to the wind instead." BWJ—June 2010

What do I mean by the *Cogito*? This is an interesting question to ponder. The cogito, I would say here, is the act of thinking on steroids. Under such conditions, the being is exploring the self in a manner that might reveal the world to him in the most fundamental ways.

I propose to examine the notion of *"Philosophizing"* with interest. I propose to shed a little bit of lights on the subject. I will hypothesize on possible techniques, which could help us assess human nature.

There is a link between *human survival* and *human Beingness*. I propose to explore that link by reflecting on the intricacies of being in the world. But I will do so from an ontological lens.

This work does not have an empirical foundation. I will cite fewer publications. Hence, the ideas projected herein are speculative in nature.

In spite of these limits, the views I will outline in this text are based on a profound analysis of the subject. I will highlight the nature of human reality. This is a discourse about human survival.

My contention is that the being must be in the world. But what is the nature of that need. Let us examine it in depth. Let us assess the implications of being in the world.

In order for the being to be, he must be aware of his *Beingness*. The being could only be aware of his *Beingness* by scrutinizing the self. To discern the self, the being must be able to think. But being able to think is not a human talent.

Every living being—be it a humanoid or else—could think. Debarring other aptitudes, human beings perform this act at the highest level. The thinking ability of a person is the basis of that individual's quest for long-term survival.

The being is not always aware of the need to preserve the self. He often becomes entrenched in the reality of his surroundings. The being might forgo his need to be by natural rights and not by chance or artificial laws.

When the being thinks, he is aware of that reality. He is able to see the world for what it is. Through the act of thinking, the being communicates with the world and with every entity in it. The world, in turn, communicates with the being. That back and forth communication is what affords the being the necessary insights about the natural milieu, which would allow him to find the means to survive beyond divine interventions or beyond providence.

Philosophy is the essence of *Beingness*. A person's ability to philosophize opens a door of unlimited insights onto nature. A person's dexterity to grasp his world in the most fundamental sense is the quintessence of his *Beingness*.

The being could philosophize by engaging in a deep conversation with the self. We could describe that conversation as the act of thinking itself. Such a state [of being] is important for the being's long-term survival. The question is what might induce that state of being? Let us explore the characteristics of a thought.

A HUMAN THOUGHT

What is a thought? I discuss this notion at greater length in chapters 4, 7, and 8. For now, let us say that a thought is an expression of a mental reflex.

A thought is as simple as recognizing an event; it is a way of acknowledging an entity; it is a way of becoming aware of one's *Beingness* or one's presence [or one's state of being] in the natural. In laying down this argument, I am aware that my contentions might not spell out the true characteristics of human thought producing.

The previous explanation is perhaps confusing. To some, it might be vague. For others, it might be illogical.

Some observers might argue that there is more to the act of thinking than relegating it to a mere physiological state of being. I would not perforce refute that view. I would concede that the act of producing thoughts generally entails an array of attributions, many of which are independent in their own way. Hence, there is no need to challenge the view that human thinking is complex.

What is a thought in the most lemon term? We could define the act of thinking as a physical or a mental nimbleness. The attribute itself involves several body parts and organs. This course of action may include the eyes, the ears, the nose, and other sensory parts inside and outside of the body. The development of a thought, at least consciously, often includes the brain, which, in turn, serves as a catalytic force for human awareness.

There is no need to examine the practical details of what makes up a thought. This work was not designed to examine the nature of human thinking in depth. Still, it will explore aspects of human thinking mechanism. That being said, this is a daunting task. Nonetheless, there is more to the production of a thought than this short collection could explicate.

There is a lot happening in the brain. The person has to process it all in order to make sense of the self. To reiterate a previous argument, the mechanism of human thinking is more complex than most people realize.

There is an inextricable link between human thinking and philosophy. Of course, this is a grandiose statement. But let us explore the notion of philosophizing closer to make sense of it all. Let us look at this idea from a broader perspective.

Introduction

SECTION I

THE NATURE OF A THOUGHT

1. THE MYSTERY OF A THOUGHT

"If existence precedes essence, then Mother Nature always precedes existence." BWJ—June 2001

A thought generally occurs at an introspective level. The being needs to go deep—some might say intensely within the soul—to understand the nature of the self. In effect, a thought is a continuous conversation the being is having with the self.

A thought could occur at a subconscious level. Under such a circumstance, the thinker is not always in control of his thoughts. But the degree to which a thought is the result of being aware of oneself is not clear. Similarly, what forms a thought is not always succinct.

The thought producing apparatus of one thinker is never obvious to someone else. Such an attribution is not evident to other thinkers. While we may know the other is thinking about something, we could not always tell when he is thinking, what he is thinking about, why he is thinking, and when he may stop thinking.

It is always a mystery to look in someone else's eyes and trying to guess what is taking place on that person's mind. Whatever we might come up with would always be our subjective understanding of what is taking place in that mind. Because of that level of subjectivity, what leads to human awareness or human consciousness is not clear.

What catapults human beings to produce thoughts is unsettled. Coincidentally, the literature is not definite about the physiology of a human thought. In this text, I will not examine the issues from such an angle.

I could only speculate about the nature of that vital human function. Arguably, no one truly knows its nature. In this case, we could assess the characteristics of a thought only from a theoretical lens.

Few people understand the intricacies of a human thought. No one individual could accurately explain what is taking place in someone else's mind. Similarly, few experts in human biology or human anatomy have insight as to the nature of a human thought.

Even connoisseurs in the field of psychology could not explain with certainty the nature of the human thinking abilities. They could only do so by relying on deductions or suppositions. This is one of the mysteries of humanness. Few could explain the process of human thinking with ease. Few could do so with great authority.

Thinking is an important feature in human beings. But humans themselves do not understand it well enough. This aspect of humanness is unsettled. It is a contested field of inquiry. This is not surprising, considering the study of human ontology is marred with controversies.

In sum, the nature of human thought producing is a debatable subject. It is a controversial issue. I do not expect to change the contentious nature of the debate by virtue of this work alone.

THE CHARACTERISTICS OF A THOUGHT

Since human thinking is not well understood, it could be difficult, if not impossible, to explain the characteristics of a thought. What amounts to a thought is not easy to make out. What we know about a thought is often the result of speculations, educated guesses, or other inferences.

Our knowledge about a thought could also be based on other beliefs, including our understanding of the brain and other organs. While I agree that such entities could be a part of the thinking process, I could not offer a precise means to explain the extent of their role in the process.

Under that presumption, I urge a bit of a reserve in your approach to the analysis presented here. I encourage you to take the views I express with skepticism. They are exploratory; they are philosophical. In that spirit, I would advise you to read this text with caution.

What is unequivocal is that there is no consensus in the debate. Our understandings about the subject are not settled. The characteristics of a human thought are not easy to decipher.

The intricacies of the human thought are difficult to explain. Because of the complexity that makes up the thinking process, people are not always able to cater a full grasp of their own thinking apparatus. What is certain is that human beings do not seek to think.

It is true that humans enjoy a wonderful thinking ability. However, they do not get out of their way to think. They just do.

The question is why that is the case. Granted, the answer eludes most thinkers. The answer eludes me as well. Withal, let us not allow our lack of imagination stop us from dissecting what is a thought or what it could be.

The act of thinking is the result of an automated dexterity. One does not learn to think. A person could not prevent himself from producing thoughts. But how could we decide the nature of the thinking

Cogito, Ergo Philosophus

instrumentality itself? This is where the lines are blurriest.

THINKING AS A HUMAN TRAIT

We are to presume that human thinking is an essential part of human *Beingness*. Even so, we could not make plain the machinery of human thought production. Short of our intellectual limitations, we still have the responsibility to disentangle the nature of a thought. We must try to achieve that goal whether or not this task is probable.

Despite the announced analytical shortcomings, I will argue that the being is always thinking. Thinking is part of being. Every living being thinks. This is true whether we are talking about a person or other living entities.

The minute the being stops thinking, he (or it) is no longer aware of the self. The being is unaware of the world around the self. The being no longer responds to any stimuli in the natural. We could describe that lack of awareness as the death of the being at the most fundamental level, if not at the molecular state.

When the being stops thinking, he is no longer a whole. The being is dead, both physically and intrinsically. The being stops to be in any manners known or imaginable by men.

13

It is not clear the degree to which humans are the only entity in nature that can produce thoughts. Many observers have argued that thinking is the trademark of *humanness*. I would not challenge this view without outlining my own construal of the issues. This is precisely what I propose in this work.

By most standards of assessment, every human being can think. It could also be said that thought producing is the essence of human *Beingness*. By that logic, it could be argued that being able to place one-self somewhere in the world is the quintessence of self-identification. That self-identity is always plain.

SPEAKING AND SELF-IDENTITY

In the human world, the presumption is that a superior being is a being that speaks. It is also believed that a being that speaks is a being that does not have any anatomical, physiological, or psychological hindrance to do so. A being that speaks is a being whose mental state is optimum. From here, a being whose mental state is at its best is a being that is in control of the self.

A being that is in control of the self is a being that lacks any limits or any form of restraints in the world. The being might be able to express his sentiments at will. Such a being might be free or has the mental means to take control of the self.

The common understanding is that human beings have the means to claim their freedom from any encroachment. This would always be true, whether or not such impediments might be physical or mental. They say that today's human beings possess what it takes to surpass their prehistoric counterparts. That is, human beings these days have the means to rule over the world.

Under any circumstances, they say, the being is free. He has the means to understand the need for freedom. Except that, such a view about human beings is absurd. While I will not address the notion of freedom at length in this work, I will say this much. It is widely accepted that the ability to speak is an indication of awareness.

Being aware of the self is a state of being or a condition, which is necessary for the being to recognize the self in the world. That recognition could be the instigator of freedom or the quest of that. The understanding is that a being that is aware of the self is a being that is free. At least, such a being has the capabilities for it.

It is also believed the ability to speak is an expression of mental competence, which means that the being that speaks has a superior intellect as opposed to the being that does not. A being that speaks is a being that thinks. A being that thinks is a being that is aware of the self in the world. A being that is aware of the self is a being that has the desire or the necessity to be free.

It is irrefutable that speaking is the quintessence of humanness in the world. It would be odd if a person could not speak. Without fail, however, there are instances where a person might not be able to speak. Sometimes, it is because of a congenital problem, which must be corrected by artificial means. The development of sign language is perhaps one of such means.

It is widely accepted that speaking aptitudes form a gauge or a clear signal of intellectual superiority. The belief is that the ability to form a communication instrument, which is audible to a point where it is both tangible and abstract, is a sign of mental pre-eminence. Leaving that understanding aside, this is not the case in all instances.

The notion of self-identity in the world is not set in stone. Such an identity, I would also contend, is not perforce expressive. Identity in the natural, I would further echo, is the knowledge of one's presence in the environment. The way one expresses that knowledge or the way one reveals that presence could be understood as a happening. Short of other natural hindrances, the aforementioned antecedent is not necessarily a precondition to be in nature.

2. THE ABILITY TO SPEAK

"Subsistence always supersedes existence." BWJ—June 2008

Many people are convinced that the ability to speak is one of the greatest features in human beings. Some observers have even tied that ability with mental prowess. Others have credited that ability to a form of superiority. I would argue that being able to speak or the lack of that is not the only indication of mental skills or the potential thereof.

Such abilities do not reveal a being's intellectual potential. It does not clarify the being's latent intellectual skills. Hence, there is more to *Beingness* itself than a mere ability to speak. In saying that, I would also admit that being able to speak appears to signal mental skill or other cognitive abilities.

One of such abilities, it could be argued, is the capability to think. A spoken word is a vocalized thought. To reiterate a previous point, our understanding of a thought is still at its infancy. Our understanding of humanness is at a primitive stage.

Our limited understanding of what a thought is or what such a function could be is the foundation of our beliefs about human intellect. Such an approach to human *Beingness* is generally mistaken. It does not provide any tangible explanation, which would allow us to judge the true nature of a person's innate abilities to be in the world.

Many observers have linked human language with human thinking abilities. Some have also attributed that ability to *human superiority* in both their world and the world of others. I would echo that being able to speak (or the lack of that) is not a sign of superiority (or the dearth of that) in any way, shape, or form.

What I am echoing here is that a human thought or a human language is not the foundation of human supremacy anywhere in the world. It is not even the case among human beings themselves. Rather, such abilities are a mere sign of being aware of oneself. They are the tell-tale-signs of humanness.

It is unquestionable that speaking is the trademark of human beings. It could also be said this is not vital for survival. Thus, the ability to speak is not a condition for the being to be. It is not a precondition for the being to maintain its existence.

Any being can be in the world. Being able to speak often has little or nothing to do with human survival. This is to say, most people would survive even without the ability to produce speech. Human beings do not have a unique way of communicating among their selves. It is irrefutable that people who are deaf (and cannot speak) have an incontrovertible sense of self in the world.

What I am trying to say is that people who are hard of hearing are attuned to their self-identity. Their mental competence can even surpass that of a *"normal"* person. By using the term normal, I am referring to those whose speaking abilities are not impeded in any way, shape, or form.

What makes it possible for a person to speak? It is the person's ability to think, I would denote. But the ability to think supersedes the aptitude to speak. A person could not speak if he or she could not think.

The perverted view is that thinking is a human trait. The problem is that the degree to which human beings are the only entity that have such a faculty is not clear. Not only every human being can [and usually does] think, any other living entities in the natural environment could do the same. For a fact, they normally do so in their own way. The challenge, I would signify here, is to provide enough evidence to support this claim beyond any doubt.

Other living beings engage in thought producing as much as human beings do it. This is the trademark of survival. The being (be it a humanoid or else) could not survive in the natural unless he or it is aware of that reality.

Awareness, in and of itself, forces the being to engage in a conversation with the self. The being often has no choice but to engage in a *Private conversation* (or a *Tête-à-Tête*) with the other entities within the environment. That conjuncture allows the being to become certain of his identity. That certainty, in turn, allows the being to strive to preserve his *Beingness*.

NO THOUGHT CONTROL

The act of thinking is not a form of human capabilities (or a role), which the being has the choice to do without. The being does not have the innate competence to heighten that attribution at any given point during the thought production. The act of thinking is part of the *Beingness* of the being.

Human beings do not always know that they are thinking. The being could not decide when to think, what to think about, and how to think about what he is thinking about at any given point during the act of producing a thought. There ought to be a trigger or some stimulant, which would prompt a thought.

The natural environment contains many of such stimuli agents. Everything in the environment incites awareness in the being. This is the trademark of the natural. But the being must become in synchrony with the natural. This is the essence of survival, I would further echo in this case.

To be in nature is to be everywhere and anywhere. Not counting other realities, a natural state of being is not limited to humanoids. When it comes to human beings, the being must be aware of his state of being all the time. From here, the human thinking agency is always at work, whether the being is aware of what is taking place in the backdrop of his mind.

Could we be certain of the degree to which other entities in the environment are aware of human beings? Could we say this is the case whether such entities are alive or in inertia? If so, what could be the implications of that state of awareness? Answers are not clear.

While it is not obvious whether inert beings have a level [or a natural state of] consciousness akin to that of human beings, there is enough evidence to suggest that every living being has some form of a conscious state. That state of *Beingness* can be obvious in the way a living being interacts with other entities in their environment, including human beings. Every living being has a soul (or a conscious state), which oversees the physical self.

Nobody knows what is happening in the consciousness of other living entities. By other entities, I am referring to animals and other living beings. We must also certify the degree to which other beings [namely animals] can think. To arrive at a satisfactory conclusion, we must first examine the inherency of a thought. In the present context, however, we could only do so by examining the thinking process of a humanoid.

THE INHERENCY OF A THOUGHT

While human thinking often occurs subconsciously, the being must become aware of the act of thinking itself. He must do so under any circumstance. The being must become aware of the thought production, at least at some point during the act of thinking. This state of awareness affords the being the pillar on which to rest his *Beingness* in the end.

The ability to think affords the being a huge advantage in the natural milieu. The being would be able to gauge the self. No holds barred, he would only be able to do so from an introspective lens. Nonetheless, the being would be able to probe the self from an outward angle.

The being would be able to see the self. He would be able to examine any perception of that self in comparison to other entities in the environment. The being would be able to probe the self in relation to entities that interact with the self directly or entities that witness the being in the environment where the being evolves. The being would be able to determine what the self is (or is not) in relation to others. The being would be surviving.

In the process of this continuous self-scrutiny, the being would become aware of his state of consciousness. The being would be able to take actions (or to omit actions) that might prolong (or cut short) his existence. In the midst of this life or death struggle, the being would find the means to survive.

That state of awareness is what I describe as *the act of philosophizing*. Howbeit, this feature is not inherent solely in human beings. Other living entities enjoy a similar state of awareness. In that sense, thinking is not a human modus; at least, this is not the case restrictively.

Other living beings think. For sure, they do so in a limited way. Notwithstanding that reality, they engage in a similar conduct. It could be argued that other living beings produce thoughts in their own way.

THINKING AND HUMAN AWARENESS

Thinking is the quintessence of *Beingness*. When it comes to a person, the being would ponder about his thoughts. The being would reflect of what he might be thinking about at any given time during his state of consciousness. The being would assess the implications of those thoughts, as they might be relevant to his *Beingness*.

Granted, the being (in this case, a humanoid) might not be aware of a thought when it occurs. A person is not automatically aware of the act of thinking. Since thought producing is almost an involuntary event, the being can become overwhelmed by the quantity of thoughts that might be traveling through his mind at any given time. Thus, the being might become selective about which thought to afford more importance.

Under any condition, the being would always be thinking. This is true since thinking is part of being. Likewise, because of that state of being, people could fall out of themselves.

The being could become unaware of his state of consciousness or the lack of that without set limits. The being could become an automated entity. Under such a condition, the being would be *vulnerable in the world*. He would also become *susceptible to the world*. The being would no longer strive to prolong his *Beingness*. The being would be *dormant*.

The being must become aware of both the self and the other entities, which could be lethal to his *Beingness*. On that recognition, the being would seek to preserve the self. If the being never reached the point where he is aware of the self, then he could stop *to be* altogether.

Resultant of that state of being, the being could mislay his essence. But such a way of being is not conducive for the being to aim toward long-term survival. The being would still be, though by fortune.

If the being were to become unable to coordinate his *Beingness* in comparison to other beings in the natural milieu, the being would effectively become a zombie. The being *would be* just *to be*. The being *would not be* because he wants to be beyond chance. Rather, the being would become an automated entity. His survival, in both the short-term and in the end, would be fortunate.

Chapter 2: The Ability to Speak

3. THE ZOMBIE EFFECT

"If you could not subsist, you could not exist." BWJ—June 2004

When the being is no longer aware of the self at the intrinsic state of being, the being could become *maladroit*. He would become *susceptible* to his own nature in the natural. I refer to this state of being as the *"Zombie Effect."* Under such a conjuncture, the being would be alive. Still and all, he would not be aware of himself in the most fundamental sense.

The being could become impervious to the danger of being. The being would be unaware of the danger of being around other beings. The being would be defenseless; he would be exposed; he could experience premature death.

The being would be at a one-dimensional level. The being would simply not be there, even though his presence, both in flesh and in the mind, could be irrefutable. The being could lack the mental presence to withstand the reality of being. The being could become absentminded.

Human consciousness is a special state of being in the world. The problem is that there is not a reliable metric to gauge such a way of being. Consciousness is a personal state of being, which is only relevant to itself.

Human consciousness only concerns the individual (or the entity) who is aware of that reality. My consciousness only concerns me. Just the same, your state of being only concerns you.

My state of consciousness is only relevant to my *Beingness*, as yours is only relevant to you. Because of the subjective nature of human consciousness, we could examine this state of being only from an introspective lens. But the human mind is best suited to discover the nature of its own state (or its level) of consciousness.

THE ACTIVE CONSCIOUSNESS

Human consciousness is an endless happening. Under such a state of being, the being is always active. Not the less, the human mind is not always aware of that state of being. Thus, consciousness is a way of being, which does not occur on its own; it could only come about with some outside [or external] stimulus.

Few people pay close attention to their state of awareness. Sometimes it is a defensive technique. The being simply does not want to carry the load of constantly striving to survive. In this case, the being wants to avoid the load of finding the best means to stay alive.

The being might feel the responsibility of living too complicated. He might find the struggle of preserving his life too burdensome. The being might succumb under the weight of trying to stay alive. The being might give up on the self.

Other times, the being might ignore his state of awareness because of the environment itself. But it might suit others that some people are unaware of their reality. The being might get to a point where he feels that he has a duty to forgo his state of *Beingness*. He might do so to the loss of his *Beingness*.

The being could find it easy to ignore his state of being. He might also do so because of some training he received. It could be because the being sees the world through the lens that others put forth before him. Under such a way of being, the being would be « *Zombifié* » or *"Zombified."* The being would be turned (or transformed) into a *Zombie*.

Most human beings evolve under a similar state of being. They often become captive of the routine of life in their milieu. As a result, they could easily become unaware of their *Beingness* in their world.

This conjecture might explain the complexity of being both *intrinsically* and *outwardly*. This reality also makes the study of thought production difficult. The presupposition in most literary circles is the notion that the being is predictable. I do not share a similar sentiment, although I agree that a being could learn to become predictable. Nonetheless, I propose a slightly different approach here.

If the being had not been aware of himself in the environment, he would become vulnerable. The being would interact with the world in a way that might not benefit his [or its] survival interests in the end. The being would lack purpose in life.

The being would be lost. He would not recognize himself in comparison to other entities. The being would be susceptible to other beings, including human beings and other beings.

The notion of philosophizing involves the idea that human beings struggle to remain in the world. Only, that struggle comes with all sorts of issues. However incredible this might sound, human beings often fail to secure the necessary means to survive. Life is an eternal struggle for survival. We could refer to this *De facto* reality as *the essence* of *Beingness*.

The *Cogito,* or the thought producing mechanism, at least as I describe it here, is the intellectual apparatus, which allows the being the presence of mind to question his reality and to examine his state of being within that reality at any given point. The act of thinking provides valuable insights to the being about the environment. I would call this environment *nature.*

That state of being allows the being the resourcefulness to gauge his role in the environment. As a direct result of that state, the being might assess the world at a different level. The being might try to frame his world as he sees fit.

That constant strive is the essence of the *Cogito.* It is the essence of survival. This is the case not just for human beings, but it is also the same for any living entity known to humanity.

A HUMAN SET UP

Philosophizing is similar to human understandings, although a few nuances are worth considering. What we do or what we omit from doing could be the result of both our innate ability to reason and based on our natural potentiality to think about the world from a meticulous prism. In this case, I am alluding to the human perspective itself. We could examine such a way of being based on our own faculty to make sense of what we think about during the thought producing itself.

Thinking, at least at a shallow level, is not exclusive to humans. We could describe the act of deep thinking as a thorough scrutiny of the self. Such a degree of understanding about the self normally takes place at the most intrinsic state of being. It is almost [only] a human affair. Until proven otherwise, there is no way around that understanding.

I must point out that the previous statement does not imply any human ownership of thought-production. As noted in interior paragraphs, every being could [and routinely does] think. I will echo this idea relentlessly throughout the remaining portion of the manuscript.

A being that thinks does not have to be a humanoid. This is to say, an entity, whether active or inert, which has the ability to engage in similar exercises, does not have to be a person. However, something curious about human beings is worth highlighting as we go along in our analysis.

A humanoid has a distinct characteristic in nature. Overtime, human beings have developed a communication medium, which appears unparalleled in comparison with anything else within the natural environment. The problem is that such an oddity is not open to the scrutiny of all. We could only understand it from a human perspective. In other words, this human peculiarity is only for other humans to make out.

Human beings are, by any seeming, the sole owner of their *Beingness*. As far as we know, only a human being could make another. Only humans have the endowment to understand themselves in the most fundamental sense.

When it comes to human beings, I do not need to speak your language to have a sense of your state of mind. By looking at you, I could convince myself anything about your frame of mind. By hearing your voice, I could speculate whether you are antagonized or perplexed. In reality, some might say, I could only pretend to know whether you are sad, angry, or happy.

Despite my insights into your state of being, I could not be certain of your intrinsic state of being. Even you (yourself) are not always certain of your own state of being. The man becomes a mystery to both himself and to others. The *Cogito* is the bridge, which affords a person the presence of mind to find himself amid the chaos of life.

Something about human beings sets them apart from other animals. Whether it is the human anatomy or the human biology, there is something inherent to being a man, as opposed to being anything else in the world. Yet, at the most fundamental state of being, no two men are alike. What might explain such a contradiction? Let us delve deeper in the debate.

MEN ARE UNIQUE IN THE WORLD

It would not be fanciful to claim that men are a unique entity in nature. Within the human species itself, there is a gross distention. Such dissimilarities, some might argue, makes everyone his own master in the natural. But such degree of liberty is often confused to mean that men are *free* in the wilderness. I disagree with that understanding. In chapters 5 and 10, I revisit the notion of *freedom* a little more, although not thoroughly.[1]

A contradiction in human beings makes it almost impossible to judge the nature of the species. A person is a mysterious entity, even to the self. Per contra, this is not necessarily the case for other living entities, distinctly animals.

It could be easier to presume an animal's state of being, as opposed to a person. When a dog barks, I could intuitively tell whether it is screaming, upset, curious, or happy. When a dog looks at me, I could

---

[1] I you wish to learn more about the concept of freedom, please see my other works on the subject, notably the text titled *Crime and Nature: Examining the Seeds of Crime in Society.*

haphazardly tell whether it is happy to see me or whether it is sad, or even upset, in which case, I would know to stay out of its way. Nonetheless, I could never be certain of the emotional condition of another human being.

While I could guess a few features about human emotions, for I hold many of them too, I always need some form of a confirmation from the person in question. Even then, I could not be certain of the true state of the mind of a person. Being certain of someone else's emotional state is a rare insight into the being.

It could be difficult, if not impossible, to detect a person's true sentiment at any given point. Even for the astute observer, it could be tricky to clarify a person's genuine state of being. But what could explain such a degree of complexities in humans? The answer is not obvious to most observers.

Such a measure of peculiarity makes humanoids a unique breed of being in the world. In saying that, I do not presume that humans are a special breed of being in the natural world. Rather, humans have their own nature within the natural. In spite of everything, there exists a few conflicting realities about human beings in the world, which we could not overlook.

In the face of our uniqueness in the world, we are similar in many ways. We also enjoy some intrinsic peculiarities. That nuance, however small it might be, makes us even more difficult to decipher.

Within the human species, we enjoy a few distinctions, which set us apart from ourselves. That being said, our dissimilarities do not necessarily make us a supreme being per se. Our uniqueness does not turn us into the owners of the world.

THE EXCEPTIONALITY OF MEN

While our exceptionality does not immortalize us in the true sense of the word itself, it provides us an edge in the natural. Human beings seemingly enjoy a way of being, which is unmatched in the natural. For instance, we have been able to leave our mark in the natural in ways that few other living beings have been able to do it.

We have been able to emblematize our presence on the planet in ways that might seem alien to other living beings. We have carved the natural landscape; we have left our imprints in places that few living entities could alter. We have developed writings. We have developed languages, arts, and music. The problem is that we have only been able to communicate among ourselves.

What we do is often relevant only to us. We are supreme only among ourselves. This reality also suggests that our *Beingness* is only consequential to our own species.

Human beings hold certain abilities, which seem unmatched in nature. Not only we can produce thoughts, but we can also suggest said thoughts by several means or through an array of channels. Human beings can transfer thoughts and feelings via a language mechanism. We could do so through art, architecture, and dance (or body language), just to name a few. As a result, we are inclined to see ourselves as omnipresent and omnipotent in the natural. But is that really the case?

It is not clear the degree to which other living creatures could think. Even so, I propose a different approach here. I will echo that all living beings must think. This is the quintessence of their *Beingness*.

We could make the argument that human beings have the potential to think at a much different—if not at a higher—level than any other living entities in the natural. In saying that, I must admit that this view is also limited in scope. It is based on our contrived understanding of the complex nature of our communication abilities (in this case, our language).

To be clear, I am not inferring that a human thought is superior to anything in the natural. I am not suggesting that humans matters the most in the universe. Let me clarify that understanding a bit further.

Chapter 3: The Zombie Effect

4. THE HUMAN FACTOR

"If being free means I have to be according to what is expected of me, then my freedom is my prison." BWJ—June 2011

Human beings seemingly enjoy an edge in the natural milieu. Some observers have credited that edge to the human thinking aptitudes. Even if that were to be the case in some instances, I could beg to differ when it comes to other situations.

A human thinking ability is only a part of the apparent upper hand the specie seemingly enjoys in the natural. Excepting that, the same abilities afford comparable benefits to other living entities in the natural world. Hence, a human thinking ability might not be an evolutionary feature in the species itself.

What might explain the nature of human beings in the natural? I am not sure. This is an open-ended question.

While human thinking abilities seem to allow the being to see the world from a specific lens, it could be said that such a perspective is available to other living entities as well. Only, the human mind is suitable for apprehending (or to see in context) the world in ways that only the bearer of a similar mind could understand. The thinking ability of the human species distinguishes human *Beingness* from other types of *Beingness*. Beyond that, there is nothing extraordinary about that ability.

The being might be able to distinguish others in two different realms. In this case, I am referring to the mind and the body. A human being could affect the self and others (or omit from doing) with both the body and the mind. This is an impressive feat, I must admit. This is why every human being could philosophize.

Thinking is probable at the most intrinsic state of *Beingness*. This is not just a human thing, even though such a feature is more apparent in human beings. Even if, what might explain that reality?

There is no definitive proof. Albeit, a likely cause is that every human being has the biological contrivance to think. Human beings hold the physiological capabilities to display that feature as spectacularly as possible.

The human being is a perceptible animal. The being has several senses, which opens the natural world to him as intensely or as profoundly as possible.[2] The being is in continuous communication with the world or a part of that, although the being is not always aware of that state of being. This is where the *Cogito* has an intrinsic value to the being.

The *Cogito* is the essentia of the being. It is so at the most fundamental level. The problem is that prominent thinkers have not always approached the concept from such an angle. In this text, I offer a different audit to examine the notion of human thinking in the most germane sense.

THE ACT OF PRODUCING THOUGHTS

While I do not think that human beings are the only entities in nature that could produce thoughts, I am not aware of any other living beings that could coherently transfer feelings or thoughts to one another, at least not in the same manner humanoids have been able to do it. When it comes to voiced thoughts, I am not sure any

---

[2] I am referring to the human nervous system. I am also referring to the sensory organs that allow the human being to assess the self in the world. Generally, those organs include the following: Sight (vision), Hearing (audition), Touch (somatosensation), Smell (olfaction), and Taste (gestation). These organs constitute the five commonly known senses of the human species.

other entities are fit for introspective thinking the same manner human beings usually engage in such office. Hence, I must accept the likelihood that human beings might be special after all.

The previous account is not a firm rejection of the possibility that other living entities, for example, animals, could engage in introspective thinking in a way similar to the way humans have the disposition to do it. I do not dispute that conjuncture at all, for I reckon that it is probable. On the other hand, we must consider the possibility that something else might be taking place.

Even if animals were to engage in such a deep state of being, we might never know it. Other living beings in the natural environment do not hold a language or any communications skills, which human beings could grasp. But that does not mean they do not have a communication mechanism or a speaking device, which is comparable to that of human beings, at least in terms of its functionality.

Most living entities in nature do not express their thoughts and feelings physically or on a tangible medium, which would be familiar to human beings. Even so, that does not necessarily deny that possibility. It does not necessarily mean they do not hold a means of communication.

The common understanding is that fewer living beings in existence today, other than human beings, could communicate thoughts and feelings to another through a tangible medium, such as a paper or a computer. Hardly any other living entities give the idea they rely solely on their communication skills to survive in their environment. Based on that understanding, one might deduce that most animals could not compare with humans in any manner whatsoever.

It is probable that only human beings hold the gift of thinking. It could be the case that only human beings enjoy the privilege of producing deep thoughts. For all that, what evidence is there, which would support such claims?

We could say that only human beings possess the skills and the aptitude to connect with nature in an intrinsic level. Unlike other entities within the environment, humans could share their connection with nature to other beings in the most tangible ways. We could describe that state of being as the act of philosophizing. To put it simply, we could refer to this function as the *Cogito*.

At this point in the debate, it is important to outline the nature of human *thinking*. It is important to understand the essence of the being by virtue of his or its capacity to produce thoughts. From this point of departure, please keep in mind that the extent of the human ontology I am trying to disentangle here is still a mystery. This characteristic of human *Beingness* is still unsettled.

What I am trying to echo in this work is that there is no definitive agreement about the nature of *Beingness*. In this instance, I am referring to a person's intrinsic ability to think. Therefore, I might not be able to speak on behalf of the human species with a great authority.

ON BEHALF OF HUMANITY

To reaffirm a previous statement, there is some undeniable uniformity to *being* a human being. For example, the human anatomy is similar. The human way of being in the world is also comparable, although there are subtle differences in human personalities. Nevertheless, it takes a human to be a human being.

I am a human being. Does that mean I could speak in the name of the human species? I do not think so.

Certainly, I could explain a few facts about the nature of humanness to another human being. I could do so without the need to go to extreme lengths. If I were to converse with another person, I might not have to explain what I mean to say after every sentence or after every word I sound off.

Certain features about being a human being are so intrinsic that only the being in question could understand them. But when it comes to awareness [or thinking], I am not sure I could be the spokesperson for another living being. That is, I am not sure I could speak for other living entities, particularly those that are close to the human species.

One could assume that occurrences (or events), which occurs in my being at the most fundamental state, take place in other human beings as well. Again, is that enough for me to speak for an entire species? I would say no.

What might explain that reality? A practical way to explain this conjuncture is that I have no clue about myself. I am ignorant about the realities of other beings. The same is true for other human beings.

The next logical question is why would I be certain that this text would enlighten you on the subject? What is it I offer that you could not make out on your own? What is it that I am saying here that you could not decipher from other writings?

I could not say this work is a reference on the subject. I could not claim it would inform you in a majestic way. In spite of its shortcomings, this work has the potential to advance the debate in the right direction.

I am not sure whether this work, on its own, would convince you that my views have some intellectual worth. Likewise, I could not even pretend the views already echoed in previous sections and the ones I will explain in following chapters could recount the reality of every living being. I could not project an authorship on ideas that you already know or ideas that you have the potential to uncover on your own. I could only speak about the human experience based on my own.

As noted before, this book is not empirical. But I offer a genuine voice about the human reality. Keep in mind this is a subjective slant about that reality. Still, this work has relevant intellectual values.

A VALUABLE CONTRIBUTION

Perhaps what I propose in this text is not that big of a deal after all. Some might say this book offers a narrow perspective about a broad topic. I would not refute that assertion.

After I made that concession, I have to mention that my goal is to take the conversation to a different, but not necessarily a refined, level. I hope to go beyond a mere regurgitation of ideas that seem to pervade the literature on the subject, which I do not deny here.

I am convinced that something else is occurring in nature. Something else is taking place in the vein of human *Beingness*. We, as intellectuals, often have a shallow grasp of it. We seldom explored that something extensively. I would like to explore this aspect of the debate as comprehensively as possible.

If you have read this work thus far, I applaud you. In the previous audits, I tried to articulate the crux of the issues I am trying to disentangle. If you are still confused, do not worry. I will elaborate further on them.

Granted, the arguments presented in this text are not detailed. My positions might not be compelling enough to sway you from one end and into another. Please bear with me, as I dissect the subject with more clarity.

Despite the noted limits, the views I will echo in the next few segments are not without merit. They do not lack cogency; they do not lack argumentative coherence. They do not lack importance. In any case, these views are worth interjecting in the literary stream.

We could examine the human experience by exploring the human flair to think. In saying that, I understand it might not be that simple. As already noted, there is no consensus in the debate.

I could not make a compelling argument about human thinking abilities when human beings are not certain about the nature of that attribution. Whatever I say would only make sense from where I stand. Of course, I might invite more dissenting views on the subject rather than furthering the debate. For these reasons, I would not take an authoritative approach in this book.

Examining human thinking is a controversial topic. I must also note that most inquirers have flushed out similar questions by examining the psychological ramifications of human thoughts. Modern medicine tends to rely heavily on deductions regarding chemical interactions in the brain to make sense of the nature of the function of that organ. I will not take a similar slant here.

While I will not take a psychological approach in this analysis about the human thinking abilities, I will address the most obvious aspects of that functionality in human biology (or human physiology). There is a need to examine these issues from a different perspective. My goal is not to make a decisive argument about the grain of human thinking.

We could examine the extent of human thought-producing inductively. Without considering, we must do so from a philosophical lens. With that frame of mind, let us explore the notion of human thought producing to make sense of its intricacies. Let us explore its ramifications a bit deeper.

5. PHILOSOPHY AND HUMAN EXISTENCE

"If it is alive, then it is thinking. If it is thinking, then it is not necessarily a man." BWJ—June 2019

From this point forward, I project to examine the reason philosophy is essential for human existence. I reckon this is not an easy issue to decipher. That being said, we could drum up this question from various angles. Notions about philosophy and human existence intertwine in many ways.

Approaching the issues from the previous angle might consume much of our stamina. It might not even be intellectually possible. Despite the limits of the positions I proposed here, my arguments will be very concise.

Philosophy is the pillar on which rests the human existence. This is the case at the most foundational state. Being able to philosophize is akin to being able to make sense of the world at a higher level. What I mean by that is the notion that the being could gauge the world introspectively.

Because of a person's innate talent to philosophize, he might be able to catch a glimpse into the world in an intimate way.[3] The being would not see the world just from a physical lens. He would be able to see his world from the most intimate prism. The being would be able to recognize the danger of his *Beingness*.

The faculty to philosophize suggests two important features about the fabric of human existence. First, philosophy involves the being in the pursuit of life. The being is not only alive, but he is also aware of the reality of being in that manner. The being is not only aware of his life, but he also has a reason to preserve it.

Overtime, the being would become aware of the danger that surrounds him in the environment. The being would become aware of the environment in ways

---

[3] Please bear in mind that I use the terms ability and capacity interchangeably. However, I am aware of their semantic distinction. I examine that distinction in a different project. For the sake of clarity, that delimitation seems rather inconsequential here.

it (i.e., the environment itself) would have never allowed any entity to make out based on a mere glimpse. The being would be in synchrony with the reality of the environment. As a result, the being would be able to carve a place where he could exist away from the treacherous nature of the natural.

The being would be able to adjust the self. He would be able to respond to the demands or the rigor of the environment. The being would not be helpless; he would not have to rely on chance to survive. The being would have a purpose. That purpose could be to find ways to go to the limit of life as long as possible.

Second, the being would be able to understand the world.[4] Only, he would not do so on the surface. The being could reflect introspectively, not just superficially. The being could imagine a world that he has yet to discover in the real world. The being could shape his natural surroundings.

The being could influence the world by behaving in a certain way. The being could either accept or reject the reality of his world. But the being would recognize that he enjoys a certain power over both himself and the entities that surround the self.

---

[4] I am referring to the world both inside and outside.

The being would be alive; he would be aware of this conjuncture at all-time. He would have the means at his disposal to find ways to be or to subsist beyond chance. The being would be that way; at least for a long time; not to mention as long as he wants it.

Note that I did not say the being would be free. There is more to freedom than relegating it to a mere want to emancipate oneself from any reality or any state of being in which one finds the self. First, the freedom itself must be available.[5]

The nature of human freedom is elusive. What is said about *freedom* or what is understood to be *free will* is not the case at all. And so, evoking the notion of self-determination to describe the human reality in the world is always farfetched. It is like appealing to a mirage to deny the existence (or the presence) of a desert.

The idea that human beings are free in the world is an inaccurate approach to the human reality. The *freedom* human beings supposedly enjoy in their world is not necessarily the case in the real world. I elaborate further on this part of the debate in subsequent chapters.

---

[5] Freedom must be available as a tangible conjuncture or a state of being in the world.

A UNIQUE APPROACH

The take away from my argument here is that philosophy is paramount for human existence. By definition, this is an unorthodox slant about the term philosophy itself. I reckon that most people have a different take on the subject. Later in the manuscript, I will demonstrate that the notion of philosophy and life intertwine in ways most people could not deny.

The being goes through life with a companion. That companion is the self. The being is in a constant communication with the self about everything he experiences in the environment. That conversation is what provides an edge to the being, as opposed to other living entities.

By being in touch with nature, the being would be able to see danger, even if that danger has yet to reveal itself to him. This state of being would allow the being to be one-step ahead in the environment. The being could learn to stir clear from both sensed and real (or dangerous) encounters.

Philosophy provides the being the practical understanding as a means to engage in the discovery of the self. Introspective thinking affords the being the necessary skills to discover his inherent abilities to see the world with the mind and not just with the eyes.

Philosophy places the being ahead of everything else in the natural.

The being could *ponder* about the self. The being could reflect on the rumination exercise itself. The being could combine the gathered information and adjust the self in the world fittingly. To do all that, the being must be able to perform the simple physiological task of thinking. But what is the best way to make out human thinking? Answers are not succinct.

There is not a convincing argument, which could challenge the notion that there exists little or epistemological understanding about human thought production. For many years, philosophers, psychoanalysts, and psychologists alike have approached the issue by exploring the nature of human consciousness. But there is no consensus to what a human consciousness entails or should entail. I do not propose an analogous approach here. Thus, I do not hope to bridge any gap in the debate.

My understanding is that human consciousness is a happening. Such an event reveals itself by an array of antecedents or events, some of which could not have taken place on their own. In any event, the human consciousness must come about because of external stimuli. Both internal and external forces must incite human awareness. Let us explore this idea a little further.

HUMAN CONSCIOUSNESS

Examining the nature of human thought producing based on the degree to which a person is conscious might not be the most practical way of exploring the nature of that state of being. A human being cannot be conscious unless that state of consciousness is the result of a series of events, which when taken together forces the entity to recognize their happening. The knowledge of the being [himself] is what I consider *a state of being* or *a state of human consciousness.*

To explain this assertion further, let us say that a person is conscious when he is aware of his state of *Beingness.* Under such a state of being, the being would realize that he is conscious. As a direct effect of that realization, the being would be able to manage his consciousness.

The being knows that he is conscious when he is able to concretize a particular state of tangible *Beingness.* The being is aware of seeing the world when he is able to open his eyes. But the being must first be able to see before he could be able to look.

Human awareness is an irrefutable state of being, which is closely interlocked with a tangible state of being or the lack of that. I know I am alive when I am certain that I am not dead. The certainty of life is the reality of witnessing other lives. Human consciousness is binding on both the *ability* and the *capacity* to be. That state of being is also about the being himself.

I could not transfer my consciousness onto another living being. I am responsible for it. I could not be certain of my *Beingness* unless I am certain of yours. Thus, a human state of being is also about the other beings within his immediacy.

The nature of human thinking is elusive. I will elaborate on that inherent human ability more concisely later. But keep in mind that I will only hypothesize about the characteristics of human thinking.

Overall, human survival begins with the simple fact of prolonging one's existence. The being must find a way to subsist beyond his existence. It is also the case that the human existence itself is dependent on a few other entities. The being must discover the self at all costs.

To discover the self, the being must engage in the pondering sequence. The being must think. See Figure 5.1 to understand the self-discovery process.

Human existence implicates a few events. First, the being must *discover the self.* Second, the being must *scrutinize the self.* This could be understood as the *Cogitation process.* Third, the being must *survive.* The survival itself is a constant repetition of the previously stated factors or events.

| Human Existence | Self-Discovery | Cogitation Process | Human Survival |

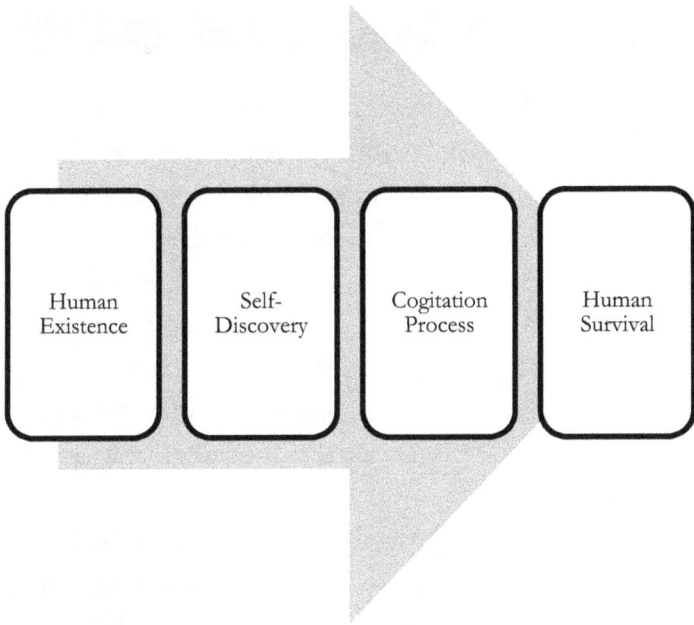

Figure 5.1: Self-Discovery

The views I foreshadowed in the previous paragraphs are distinctive in their own ways. Surely, I have taken an unorthodox gimmick in order to explain the nature of the term philosophy. The question is whether that subtlety is enough to stir you in the right intellectual path.

You could either accept or reject the views I echoed here thus far. But I would prefer that you engage this text even more. Let us venture a bit deeper in the debate.

THE NATURE OF HUMAN EXISTENCE

What is the nature of human existence? I am not sure how to address this question. At least, I do not know how to do it objectively here. What is certain is that human existence is possible through self-discovery.

Self-discovery requires a certain state of self-awareness. Omitting, that state of self-awareness is only possible through a continuous channel of communication between the being and other beings in the environment. This is what I consider the act of pondering.

The pondering procedure or the pondering instrumentation, as I argue here, is important for a prolong state of survival. Human survival is the quintessence of human existence (Refer back to Figure 5.1). The being could not exist, unless he could preserve that existence beyond chance.

In any event and under any condition, the being must survive. From within, the being must do so above all else. In it lies the essence of being. In it lies the essentia of my arguments as well.

ASSESSING HUMAN EXISTENCE

We could assess the nature of human existence in a five-step thought producing process. First, the being must be able to think. I refer to this feature as the *Cogitation*. The act of thinking is a biological attribute, which every living entity should be able to perform. Every being does so with ease.

Second, the being must be aware of the self. Through the *pondering* exercise, the being discovers the self. The being learns about the self. The being also learns certain realities about the self that might not have been obvious to him. The being knows of his existence through certain biological attributions and physiological roles.

Third, the being must be aware of the environment. As a result, the being would be able to see the world and make a clear distinction between the self and other entities in the milieu. The being would know that he is not a tree. He would understand that he is neither a bird nor an elephant.

The being would recognize the danger of drowning in the river. He would be aware of the dangerous nature of other beings in the environment where he lives. The being would become a survivor.

Forth, the being must be aware of the self in the environment. In this case, the being would understand certain ramifications or certain implications, which are intricately related to being in the natural haunt. For instance, the being would know that *Lions* eat people. The being would always be aware of the danger of facing a ferocious *Lion*.

The being would be aware of other entities in the milieu. The being would know that, while some of these entities might be visible, others might not be that obvious. Here, I am referring to entities that could affect the being, at a molecular state (e.g., a bacterium, a virus, or any other pathogens).

This back-and-forth could eventually destroy the being. At most, the being would become aware of that reality. But the being must find the means to stay clear from that conjuncture. He must do so at all costs.

Finally, the being must adjust himself in his world. He must do so according to the rigor of the environment. The being must be aware of others within the hearth. This is the only way to guarantee his long-term survival (*see* Figure 5.2).

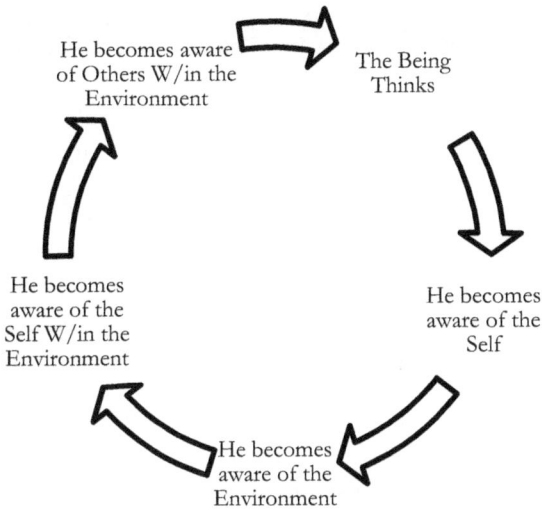

Figure 5.2: Human Existence

Could we say the previous depiction is a fair assessment of the being? I would say yes. But I am aware this is not a scientific scheme in order to examine the crux of the issues. It is not a proven modus to examine the nature of human *Beingness*. It has some significant flaws, which might compel further analysis.

The problem is there are fewer ways available in order to explore the characteristics of human *Beingness* itself. The previous explanations provide an intellectual foundation (measurably in principle) to sketch the stamp of the being. Even so, you might be reluctant to agree with my setup. I would understand the possible reason(s) for your hesitation.

A PERSONAL EXPERIENCE

What is philosophy? Early in life, I struggled with that question. For a good portion of my existence, I thought philosophy was an aesthetic mode of being or a skill, which could be learnt.

While I was in high school, I had a heated discussion with my classmates about the *manner or the nature of being* (e.g., the nature of human *Beingness*). During the class discussion, several of my classmates argued that philosophy is the art of survival. A philosopher, they said, is a survivalist by trade. Likewise, anyone could become a philosopher, they argued.

No doubt, my friends had a down-to-earth approach to the idea of philosophizing. I, on the other hand, had a more conservative view. I did not think anyone could be a philosopher.

The understanding is that philosophy is the mechanism through which a human being could become aware of the self in the world. That self-discovery, in turn, would allow the individual to assess the world for what it is and not based on how it is projected to him. Philosophy, they argued, is a portal onto a world that few could appreciate.

I did not understand the term philosophy that way. I was reluctant to view the world (i.e., the human reality, for lack of a better term) from such a viewpoint.[6] I thought about the concept of philosophy as mental prowess, which very few possessed.

At first, I disagreed with the way my classmates defined the term philosophy. Over the years, however, I realized this was a good way of approaching the underpinnings of human *Beingness* in the world. I had to change my perspective.

My reluctance to analyze the term *philosophy* from a rudimentary slant had its merit. My views were not mistaken. My concerns about the way my classmates approached the term were well founded. Your concerns about the views echoed in this work might be correct as well.

You might ask whether I should examine the term *philosophy* the way that I am doing it. You might also wonder whether I have trivialized the term to a point where it is lacking of its true essence. You might question whether I have done away with the intellectual relevance of the term itself. You might ponder on these issues, even after reading this text. I hope the next

---

[6] See the text titled *"My Philosophical Roots"* to learn more.

section would help sum up the essentiality of my arguments.

SECTION II

CHARACTERISTICS OF A THOUGHT

6. WHAT IS A THOUGHT?

"To be free on earth is to be an Alien on the planet." BWJ—June 2007

A person's ability to think could eventually become the engine of his choice for selecting survival strategies. So long as the being does not have a physiological impediment or a pathological default, any human being could think. By that logic, it could be said that every human being could engage in such an axiom. This is to say that every human being would do so with ease.

The question becomes to what extent this is true for every other being (not necessarily a humanoid) on earth. The answer is not always obvious. Exclusive of that, it is worth noting that most people believe the ability to think is only a human reality.

This approach is the result of popular, but also mistaken opinions about the essence of human *Beingness*. I do not agree with that understanding. Let me elaborate on the reason for that view.

THE NATURE OF HUMAN THINKING

It would be mistaken to argue that only human beings could think. Humans are not alone in the wilderness. The act of being in the world forces the living entity to be aware of its surroundings. Awareness in and of itself forces the being to think.

Whether the being is a humanoid or else, he/it needs to be aware of the environment. This is essential for the being to survive in the milieu itself. The being must think. Therefore, thinking is an intrinsic state of being in every living being.

While I share the belief that every human being can think, I am not sure that we are the only species that can do so. By contrast, I am certain that thinking is the essence of the being. Still, I am convinced that other living beings do it; perhaps they do it in their own way and according to their own living conditions or based on their existential realities.

Keep in mind that I am not making the irreconcilable argument that a universal thinking machine influences the living rituals of every being—mostly the ones that breathe air in the same way human beings do it—at least on this planet. Although most human beings can [and often do] think, it is not self-evidently the case that the act of producing thoughts is the same for every living being. We could not say that, at least with certainty, human thinking is akin to the thinking qualities of other living beings.

To sketch out the previous assertion further, we could say that humans do not just think. They sometimes express their thoughts in ways that only another human being could understand. They also have a tendency to do so at the most intrinsic level.

We could not say the same for other beings (in this case, I am referring to a tree or an animal). We could not communicate with them. This is probably not because they lack a communication means, which we could relate to. Rather, it is perhaps because we lack the means to know how they communicate among themselves. That is perhaps the reason we could not communicate with them.

HUMAN LANGUAGE

Granted, human beings have a natural inclination to transfer their thoughts through a complex communication instrument. We could describe this medium as *language*. Barring, this feature also makes deciphering the roots of human thought producing complicated.

Human beings are not an open book. The human mind holds many secrets. As a result, it might be difficult, if not impossible, to understand the degree to which other living entities engage in such an operation, for we have no clue about our own thinking mechanism.

I could guess what a *Dog* is thinking when it is barking at a stranger. I might be able to suggest what a *Lion* is thinking, as it chases a *Zebra* in the savanna. I could find out what a *Kitten* wants when it starts to purr, while sitting on my lap.

Despite my possible insights into the inner thinking of an animal, such as a *Lion* or a *Cat*, I could never suggest what another human being is thinking. I could never even guess what a person is thinking at any given point during a conversation or in other contexts. This is true even if that person were to tell me what is on his/her mind.[7]

The human thought is a continuing conversation among the *"being,"* the *"self,"* and the *"self-within-the-self."*

---

[7] Perhaps I could know what a person is thinking if there were a machine that could pick human vocal sound, even when they are not audible to the human ears. After all, this is perhaps what a thought is. Perhaps it is a frequency-sensitive conversation between the being, the self, and the self-within-the-self.

That conversation changes erratically and sporadically throughout the thinking process (*see* the text titled *"The Being in the World"*). Even the being [himself] is not always certain of what is taking place in his mind.

What is irrefutable is the understanding that a human being is constantly striving to make sense of the self; he is restlessly seeking to make sense of others as well. When it comes to the ability to transfer awareness, I could see why only humans show every sign of enjoying such a faculty. The presumption is that only humans have a tangible means to transfer their thoughts.

Our understanding of what a thought is (or what it could be) is mistaken. We assume that a thought suggests a language. Since we know of no other living entities, which hold a language similar to human beings, the belief is that only humans have the natural skills to produce thoughts. Leaving that view aside, there is more to a thought.

A language is not necessarily the forerunner of a thought. Perhaps, such a feature [or such a tool] is only a signal of a thought. We could make the case that a language is simply a medium through which a thought becomes obvious. It is perhaps a way to come about a specific state of being at a moment or time.

If you do not speak the language, you might not be able to make out the thought of the entity who is communicating with you or with another entity by such a medium. Aside from that reality, in and of itself, does not mean that a living entity that is lacking of a recognizable language is also lacking of the smarts, the ability, or the capacity to think. Hence, there is more to thought producing than we could fathom with the naked eyes.

A human ability to think seems to represent the foundation of human language itself. All the same, when it comes to other forms of communication, the degree to which human beings could understand the degree to which other living beings communicates with one another remains uncertain. [8] Even though other mammals, such as *Elephants* and *Dolphins*, give enough reason to believe they have developed a language, which allows them to communicate among their respective species, the pervading belief is that only humans have a well-developed language.

I do not challenge the understanding that only humans have a neatly structured communication medium. I do not question the extent to which humans have mastered their ability to think. That being echoed, I am skeptical that only human beings could transfer their thoughts via a tangible means.

---

[8] I am referring to a linguistic mechanism.

At this point in human history, some of the most striking questions we tried to discover about the savor of human thinking and the scope of human *Beingness* in the world remain unanswered. What makes up a thought is not clear in most literary circles. How human beings think is also unsettled.

Let us explore these ideas a little bit deeper. Let us also revisit popular understandings about the nature of human *Beingness*. Let us further assess the issues from a different lens.

NATURE PRECEDES EXISTENCE

If we were to look at the issues based on an existentialist paradigm, we would have to echo the understanding that nature precedes existence. [9] Most observers are convinced that human existence, at least from a more expanded angle, is dependent on a person's ability to subsist. The problem is the being could only be in a few ways. Withal, such ways are not subject to interpretations; nature already determined them. Thus, we could only uphold them.

---

[9] See the text titled "Nature Precedes Essence" to learn more about this understanding.

The being could only be, so long as nature allows him to be. Howbeit, for the being to subsist, he must preserve his *Beingness*. The being must preserve his physical integrity. He would do so by protecting himself from physical injuries or harms. The being must nourish the self (by eating food) regularly.

The being must preserve his mental state. He must avoid emotional distress and other mental conflicts. The being must remain sane at all-time.

The being must *reflect about the self in the world itself*; that is, as long as he wants to exist by right and not by chance. The word *ponder* (at least as I explain it in this manuscript) simply means the being is entertaining an infinite conversation with the self. In any case, the being must engage in a conversation with the self in a constant loop. That conversation is essential to further the human existence in the end.

What I am trying to put into words here is the notion that, for the being to exist beyond chance, he must preserve himself in the environment. He must do so relentlessly and religiously. This is the only way for the being to protect the self from dangerous entities or potentially life-threatening events.

In every moment and by any means, the being must be aware of the self. This is the best way for the being to avoid potentially fatal battles with entities that might seek to seize his *Beingness*. The being must become a *survivalist*.

As the being finds the self within the natural setting, he learns about nature. He also learns about his own nature during the act of thinking. As a result, the being might size up the entities that might be dangerous to his *Beingness*. The being understands his fragility in the environment, whether it be the natural world or the social environment.

The being wants to subsist. In spite of that desire, the being must first become aware of the dangerous nature of his world. He must also realize the frail nature of his *Beingness*. The being must be aware that subsistence is the key to his existence. Because of that awareness, the being must try to find the means to subsist at all costs.

The being must understand the reason he must be. This is the only way for him to preserve his *Beingness* in the end. The being must grasp his purpose. That purpose is to be in the world at any cost and in any way possible or feasible.

A search for existence is intertwined with the person's ability to think and his capacity to foresee the environment where he lives. Human existence is relative on the person's ability to decipher nature. For all that, nature always precedes human existence.

Put differently, nature precedes human *Beingness*. Humanness itself must rest on the natural to thrive. This is to say, humanness does not rely on the artificial. The milieu is a conjuncture, which the being learns to carry the self in it. As a direct effect of that reality, it is irrefutable that nature also precedes essence at all-time and in all places.[10] Saying otherwise is a misguided audit about the world around us.

We could not be outside the scope of the natural environment. We are the product of the natural. Therefore, we could only find out about our essence from the essence of the natural world itself, assuming we are open to finding such essence based on common sense.

CONVERSING WITH THE SELF

A thought is an internal conversation, which is audible or perhaps recognizable only by the entity that is engaging in such an exercise. We could describe human awareness as an internal conversation that never ends. What might seem like a simple act of a sublingual conversation with the self could also be a sign of self-awareness. The being always has the ability to become aware of the self within the environment.

---

[10] See the text titled *"Nature Precedes Essence"* to learn more about this understanding

There is a well-orchestrated structure to the conversation the being entertains with the self. A person knows that he is alive when he tells himself this is so. All you have to say to yourself is that, *"I am alive!"* The ability to oversee the self, under any circumstance, is what tells the self, oftentimes, about the existence of that self.

When a person converses with the self, that individual is taking part in two important antecedents (*see* Figure 6.1). They are not necessarily in a chronological order. These occurrences might help the being preserve the self under any circumstances in the world.

First, the person is telling the self glaringly about the self. Second, the person might assess the self. He might be able to do so as thoroughly as possible during the act of assessing the self. Those occurrences form the crux of *"human introspection."* That introspective state of being allows the being the capacity to be aware of the self, which in turn might cause the being to seek to preserve his *Beingness* (*see* Figure 6.1).

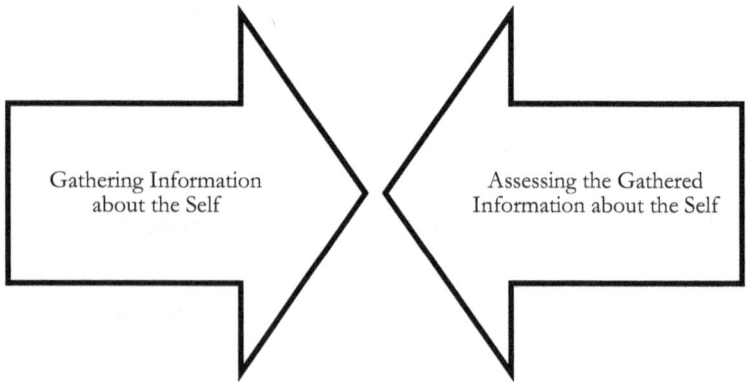

Figure 6.1: Human Introspection

As the being becomes entrenched in a deep conversation with the self, he might become aware of two instances. Here, I am referring to the being *himself.* I am also referring to the *environment* around the being. That conversation often forces the being to assess his reality from an introspective perspective.

Once the being has gathered the necessary information about the natural setting, he might make or take actions that would be in accordance with that reality. Every action (either taken or omitted) would go toward enforcing the notion that the being must protect the self. Such action or omission would always heighten the being's natural want to protect the self (*see* Figure 6.2).

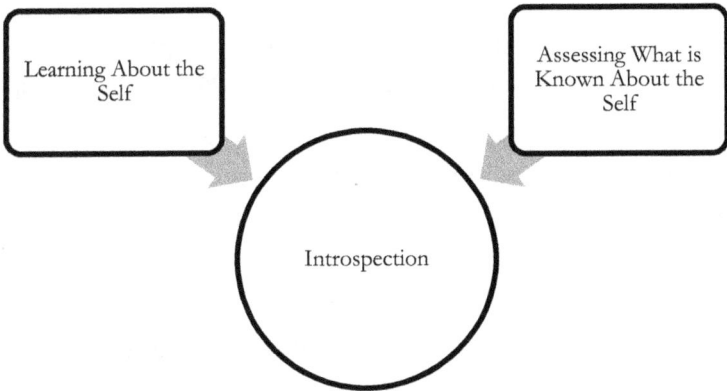

Figure 6.2: The Introspection Process

The being *ponders* as a means to reflect on the self. This act often affords the being the ability to reflect about the world at large as well. The being *Cogitates* to get to a state where he is philosophizing.

The being thinks so he could be without any set limits. To put it in a more familiar terminology, I would say *"Cogito, ergo Philosophus."* In other words, *"I think, therefore I philosophize"* (*see* Chapter 10 for more elaboration on that idea).

THE CAPACITY TO PHILOSOPHIZE

Every human being has the potential to philosophize. The question is why is that the case? The reason could not be more obvious.

The capacity to philosophize is because every human being can think. Philosophy is important for the continued existence of the species. Being able to philosophize, I would also say, is essential for human progress. This state of being simplifies the human cause.

If I were to leave the previous statement unexplained, you might think that I am just putting words on this document willy-nilly. The argument could also be made that, without the being's aptitude to forestall the environment, the being (he or she) could be exposed (unnecessarily, I might add) to all sorts of calamities. We could say the same about society.

Being aware of nature is essential to further a person's existence in his environmental setting. Again, the same is true for a social environment. The problem is that it could be more difficult for the being to be aware of the self, at least in a social setting.

Suppose you find yourself in an environment where an angry mob is about to attack you. What would be the best reaction to avoid the prospect of facing imminent lynching? The right answer might depend on an array of factors. We could also agree that it might depend on the individual [himself] or his view of the danger that he might be facing.

For some people, running away might be an alternative. For others, finding a good place to hide might be a better strategy to survive. There are also those who might try to talk their way out of the confrontation.

To explain this assertion further, we could say some people might try to convey to the mob that they are not hostile. For that reason, they deserve pity. That technique might work. There is the likelihood that such a strategy might backfire.

Negotiating with an angry mob could incite them to hurt you. Your strategy to reason with them could excite them to hurt you even more. Therefore, the being must act under the reality that he faces at any given point. Finding one's way out of a dangerous confrontation might depend on both a person's ability to sense danger, which he or she might be experiencing and that individual's wherewithal to navigate the reality that he faces.

Chapter 6: What is a Thought?

7. NAVIGATING THE WORLD

"Savagery is intrinsic in men. It could never be learnt; it could never be forgotten." BWJ—June 2018

Human survival could be dependent on the individual's potency to navigate the world. The problem is that holding the necessary appetency to navigate the world is not something the being learns vicariously. Rather, it is a natural aptitude, which every being holds.

Nonetheless, such an aptitude is not automatic. The being must learn to develop that aptitude overtime. That development, in and of itself, is a skill the being could only build up overtime. This is possible during the individual's lifetime or life experiences.

As a person matures, he or she develops the mental dexterity and the physical abilities to make out his or her own reality. The person might be able to remove the self from that reality. That shrewdness, in turn, might afford the person the necessary wisdom, which might allow him or her to adapt and adjust in his or her environmental reality. Once again, this is the essence of the *Cogito*.

Suppose a pack of hungry *Wolves* or a herd of *Lions* surrounds you. All hints suggest that they would like to gulp you down. Would you consider negotiating with those animals?

Some people might say yes. Others might say no. At any rate, it might come down to personal experiences.

Let us say you are used to animals that have the habit of yielding to human commands. In this case, you might seek to warn the vicious animals that surround you to not attacking you. You might say *"get out," "go away,"* and *"back off."*

Suppose that you are familiar with wild, but tamable, animals, such as a wild *Horse*. You might be inclined to order some of the wolves or the fiercest *Lions* of the herd to *"stand down,"* as if the animal would understand your commands.

Suppose you have seen these animals in action. You know they would attack you no matter what you do or do not do. As a result of that experience, you might have a different maneuvering.

You might run as soon as you realize the danger. You might climb a tree or you might grab a branch or something to defend yourself. The question becomes, why would you say no to the possibility of negotiating your way out of trouble if you are dealing with a bunch of hungry animals?

For most people, the answer is obvious. You could not reason with wild beasts. Such animals respond to their instincts. That is, they do not make out the world as we do it. There is some well-founded wisdom to that viewpoint.

An important contradiction is worth pointing out in this reflection. The common understanding is that wild animals are not aware of themselves like we do it. They are not aware of the environment in the same manner that we do. We describe what animals do or what they omit from doing as an intrinsic reflex to the world around them.

While human beings reason, other beings, notably animals, do not, they say. The inference here is that whatever animals do, they do it by reflex or instincts. This view is, in all likelihood, not the case at all.

THE CAPACITY TO REASON

Every bearer of life can reason. There is no way to challenge that argument. There is enough evidence in nature to suggest that, if human beings can reason, so could any other living entities.

If the end of life is death, then the logical conclusion is that birth is the beginning of life. When the being is born, he must be able to preserve his life. He must do so under any circumstance or by any means.

Anything that is alive must stay alive; at least that entity must strive to stay alive at all costs. This is the essence of existence itself. The bearer of life must subsist. This is the only way for the being to preserve his (or its) existence.

The question becomes how to stay alive? The only possible answer is to avoid death. To avoid death, the living entity must understand what death is and what it represents for his [or its] *Beingness*. To arrive at that conclusion, the being must also be able to rationalize both life and death, at least as separate realities. The being must have the ability, the capacity, and the faculty to reason.

By that logic, we could not limit reason to a human feature. This is to say, every living being understands the need to survive. Every living being thrive to survive. By extension, whether a humanoid or else, every living being can reason. For the same reason, every living entity can philosophize.

Certainly, there are degrees of reason. There are degrees of philosophizing. On that front, human beings enjoy an edge over other living entities, at least in their own world. By that understanding, I mean they enjoy a few advantages outside the natural environment itself. In this case, I am referring to a social milieu. A likely way to explain that understanding is by referencing a human language.

Even though an animal might not have a language, which a human being could grasp, that does not mean that wild beasts could not reason. For this reason, we could not say animals could not think. My contention is that wild animals think in the same manner that human beings do it. Cardinally, they might do so to the extent of their thinking abilities. In any event, such capabilities, I am trying to echo here, might be different from humanoids.

This is to echo that animals have the ability to reflect about themselves. By inference, it could also be said that they have the faculty to reason. Except that, one might say, they do so in their own way. Put differently, they do so according to their own nature.

The nature of the natural itself is what makes it natural. The notion that savagery is against nature is a misguided way of looking at the world. The wilderness is the natural. The natural is the normal.

Granted, not everything enjoys such a capacity or state of being neither in nature nor in society. Not everything in nature is alive at the same level. It is irrefutable that the natural state of being applies to every living and breathing entity in any milieu, be it social or else.

NATURE IS WILD

I agree that nature is savagery. Most living entities within that environment are wild; they respond to their inherent instincts to survive. In this case, the term instinct does not differ from the notion of reason.

To these animals, a person is just another meal or another prey. For some animals, reputably a *Chicken*, a person is just another predator. Just the same, a wild animal could not ignore the human presence in its surroundings, especially when it is hunting for food.

When a human being faces a pack of wild animals, the best—if not the only—strategy to remain alive is to run for safety.[11] Many a time, the animal already has a plan in motion to appropriate the person. Sometimes, the animal reacts or acts as a defense mechanism. Other times, the animal reacts or acts in the fulfillment of a well-devised strategy. Sometimes, it is an offensive mechanism, which was conceived to survive or to eliminate a threat to its survival.

---

[11] I am not advocating the person to run willy-nilly. The being must have a sense of why he is running.

In many cases, whether a person is faced with a single animal or a pack of wild animals, the best reaction is to find a means to escape from the danger zone. That reaction might be important to preserve one's *Beingness* in the end. Outside anything else, this reaction might also be inherent in all living entities on planet earth.

Unless they possess the natural dexterity to defend the self, most people or most living being would run for their lives in the face of danger.[12] Sometimes, the ability to run is a defense mechanism. But why there is the notion that human beings are different from other living entities in the natural setting? I am not sure where this understanding emanated.

There is nothing in nature, which would suggests that we might be the only being fitted for preserving our *Beingness* in that environment. Likewise, there is no sign that human beings lack savage traits. Civilization could not derail nature in the being. Living in society does not do away with our intrinsic ability to be humans.

As human beings, we are animals. We are wild entities. And so, we might be conducive to responding

---

[12] See the Oxford Reference to learn more about this concept. Reference Oxford, "Fight-or-Flight Response - Oxford Reference," accessed January 4, 2018, http://www.oxfordreference.com/view/10.1093/oi/authority.20110803095817447.

to our nature in the most naked manner and an intrinsic way. This is to say, we are savage beings as well.

Just like a pack of *Wolves*, we could be as lethal for another human being, eminently when we conglomerate as an angry mob. Underneath our so-called civilization, we are as savage as the *Lions*. We are lethal for our own species as any virus could be. Thus, we are not different from a bacterium, which could devourer our flesh.

We could be as treacherous as the wilderness. No matter what, our bestiality is natural. Even if we normally evolve in a controlled milieu, we are always under the influence of our nature.

To be clear, I am not suggesting there is anything wrong to that reality. After all, we are humans; we are animals; we are savages. No one has offered any evidence to challenge that understanding. In other words, over the course of human history, no one has sought to disprove this view.

The reality is that we seldom recognize our bestial nature. This is why we are likely to seek to tame ourselves in the natural. This is also the reason we often become a threat for our own survival.

Certain attributes about human beings seem a bit odd. We carry ourselves as if we were the only entity on planet earth fitted for reflecting about our nature at the most intrinsic level. The question is why this is the case. Presently, answers are not clear. That is why we have no clue about which we are, who we are, where we came from, and where we are headed.

HUMAN NATURE AND SOCIAL JUNGLE

Human beings have a wild side built-into their soul. The question worth asking here is why we are inclined to lean toward reacting to our environmental reality differently. That is, as opposed to a *Lion* or a *Tiger*.

Why do we represent ourselves as if we were the only ones capable of enjoying the moxie to control our nature? Why we pose ourselves as Gods? But is there any shred of evidence to support our hubris? Are we really omnipotent? Are we omnipresent? I would concede that I am not sure how to answer these questions.

No matter what we think of ourselves, we could understand this reality as a mistaken racket about ourselves. This is a misguided way of assessing the essentiality of human *Beingness* in a world that is so precarious for human beings. We are nothing but a breath of air. Short of that, we are a pile of dust. Thinking that we are Gods is a misreading about the domain of our nature. Thinking that we are wireless beings is arrogant and dangerous. Human beings cannot control their nature.

In spite of everything I have echoed in anterior segments, I reckon that human beings have a different nature within the natural. This is true in relation to a vicious *Lion* or a *Tiger*. Even so, human beings are as wild as any other animals in the natural environment. To reiterate a previous statement, we are animals as well.

We are only good at camouflaging our wild side, when it is unnecessary to expose ourselves. While we do not have the majestic power of a *Bear*, which would enable us to overpower a *Lamb*, we do have the cunning of a *Fox* to create a means, which would enable us to overpower both a *Lamb* and a *Bear*. By that logic, we are not different from other living entities in the natural.

Despite our reality in the world, we call ourselves *Intelligent Beings*. From that phrase alone, we could make out our recognition of our ability to think. But that view also supplants us on the pinnacle of life itself. From our vantage point, we use our *"Intellect"* or our brainpower to catapult us in the natural.

Since we have an inclination to outsmart most animals in the natural setting, we assume that they are not as smart as we are. We often become so overwhelmed by our hubris that we are now certain that most animals have no intelligence at all.

We have de-naturalized other living beings in the natural environment. We tend to play God when it comes to which animals deserve to carry through. We decide which ones must perish. We have lessened most living entities to a mere happening in the wilderness. We view their lives as being inconsequential to our own purpose, as if we owned them.

Human beings have placed themselves in the apex of life. Be that as it may, do we belong there? I am not sure. In saying that, I reckon that any answer provided could be controversial. Who we are or what we are in the wilderness is not settled.

Some people could argue that *Self-determination* is likely the reason human beings are on top of the world. But are we really on top of the world? Do we really dominate nature? I would say no.

We certainly have the apperception to overpower most living entities in nature. We also have the capacity to overpower ourselves. It follows that we have a limited impact on the natural. On a large-scale, for instance, our knowledge to influence *Mother Nature* is ephemeras and inconsequential, for we are wired to self-destruct.

We have an incommensurable impact on our own species in the natural milieu. However, our strength is in both our numbers and in our intrinsic capacity to communicate with nature in ways that few living entities ever could. What we do in nature affects us (as a species) at the most fundamental level.

We enjoy the mental and the physical dimensionality to affect nature, although in a limited way. We often see ourselves as the landlords of the planet. This is what we think of ourselves. We think we are superior. Yet, this would only be the case in comparison to other living entities. Nonetheless, there is an indisputable reality between what we think of ourselves and who we truly are in the natural milieu.

While we think of ourselves as the owners of the world, we are also aware that we have little or no power over the world at its intrinsic state of being. If not, we know that we could only alter our view of the world and not the world itself. We are aware that nature rules.

NATURE ALWAYS RULES

Human beings (both in groups and as individuals) have little or no significance in the natural environment. While as a group we enjoy a survival edge over most living entities, as a unit we are vulnerable as an ant. All the same, our vulnerability is not just in the natural environment, it is also obvious in the social environment as well.

To restate a previous argument, within the natural environment, human beings can be powerful as a group.[13] All the same, humans could be untamed and

---

[13] See the text titled *Owners of the World.*

unstoppable in the social pad. Nonetheless, when it comes to finding a means to changing our fate in nature, we seem clueless.[14]

Men could not outrun nature; they could not thwart their eventual mortality in it. So long as men live in the natural haunt, they will perish in it. There is no way out of this conjuncture. The reality is that there is nowhere else to go. There is nowhere else to be outside nature itself. Therefore, it is irrefutable that we are the subjects of our nature; it is not the other way around.

Human beings could not find a way to undo nature. We could not reverse the emprises of *Mother Nature* over our nature. Perhaps we could change parts or aspects of nature. Withal, that does not mean that we could alter nature altogether.

Indeed, we could stall our mortality in nature. Except that, we could not stop our eventual death in the natural. Despite our [obvious] capacity to influence nature, we must perish in it. Thus, we die in nature so that other beings could thrive in it.

When a man dies, countless of other beings are born out of him. Some of these being are born inside the rotted flesh of the dead man, while other parts of that flesh are still alive in ways the human mind could not

---

[14] See the text *We Have No Clue.*

understand. The new life that springs out of the decayed living entities is often paramount for the existence of other living entities. By that logic, there is no death in nature.[15]

In the face of our dependence on the natural environment, we could also affect nature in a way that seems irreversible. We could harm the natural in ways unimaginable. Over the last few years or so, we have been able to affect the natural milieu in ways that previous generations of men could not fathom.

In spite of the previous recognitions, I could also make the case that nature granted us the reach to do whatever we desire to do. Perhaps we are part of a grand design, which nature put in motion so we could fulfill its final wishes. But what that might be. Of course, I could not certify to that conjuncture beyond any doubt, for I am not sentient to Nature's final plans for humankind.

What is undeniable is that nature will always have the advantage in the natural milieu. No matter what, nature will always be in control of its creations, including us. The notion that human beings dominate nature is

---

[15] Death is only a temporary state of being. It is another stage of being in the world, which must culminate in the birth of countless of other beings. I elaborate further on this idea in another book project.

farcical, to say the least. But where that view emanated, I wonder? Well, I am not sure how to answer.

There are no specific explanations in the literature, which might help us pin point the origins of that idea. One could argue that this is a way for us to satisfy our ego. This is perhaps a way for us to encourage ourselves to strive to survive before the huge, at times, impossible, task of being in the world.

Deep inside, we know that we control nothing in the natural setting. We control no one, but ourselves. We are insignificant, for we have given ourselves no tangible significance.

Our accomplishments only raise to the level we understand it. We are who we think we are. Notwithstanding that conjectural reality, whoever we think we are might not necessarily be who we truly are.

We are perhaps nature's most inconsequential beings, at least when it comes to the larger scheme of what is taking place in the cosmos. We cannot deny the fact that nature rules us. We could not refute that the natural would always rule our world.

We resort to dishonesty to justify our ignorance of our reality. We create religions or illusory divinities to justify our shortcomings in the world. We lie to ourselves. We deceive ourselves. We are disingenuous.

Chapter 7: Navigating the World

SECTION III

THINKING AND HUMAN DOMINATION

8. HUMAN DOMINANCE IN NATURE

"Whenever you ask for something that might make you happy, chances are you would not get it." BWJ—June 2012

The human strength in the natural environment is akin to that of an ant or an ant colony. We are as fragile as we are strong. Therefore, the extent to which we are different from other living entities in nature remains a mystery.

We think we are superior in our world. Nonetheless, we have no tangible ways of being certain of that likelihood beyond the reach of our physical domains. We are certain of nothing beyond our need for certainty.

From a more practical standpoint, we know that we are vulnerable. Still, we have no certainty about our nature. We do not know who we are in the natural surroundings. We are unkind to our kind.

Instead of being humble, we are likely to adopt a pretentious attitude toward ourselves. We think that war is the only way to get our way. We are disposed to obliterate ourselves to preserve our ideals about whom we think we are. We are civilized savages.

We are a threat to our own humanity. We are puny; we are vein. We prioritize the mundane; we trivialize anything that put in question our sanity. We are lost; we are humans.

In truth, we wonder around the wilderness in the search of meanings about ourselves. But before the immensity or the magnificence of the world, we often grow even more insecure about ourselves. We lose ourselves as a way to find it wherever that self might be. This could explicate the reason we seem so lost in the wilderness.

Because of our lack of certainty about ourselves and everything else around us, we live in constant fear. Deep down our soul, we know that we are inconsequential. We also know that we have certain skills, which seem unmatched in the environment. And so, we are aware of both our existential necessity and our existential irrelevance.

This realization often leads us to shore up ourselves. We refuse to admit our existential irreverence. Within our *Beingness*, we are aware of our irrelevance or inconsequence on the map. As a result, we live in an existential paradox.

On the one hand, we know that the world is within reach. On the other hand, we also know that we could not own it. We are aware that we have no proctorship on nature. We can only claim ownership of nature.

We are aware that not even nature owns the natural environment. The world would not allow us to seize it. Instead, the world owns us, both body and soul.

I debate the ontological significance of human *Beingness* later in the text. Keep in mind that I do not dole out the final answer to the questions I posed here. I recognize that few could provide convincing explanation about any probable distinctions between humans and other living beings.

To understand a *Monkey*, one would have to be a *Monkey* oneself. Short from that conjuncture, one could only speculate about the reality of *Monkeys*.[16] Exclusive of that reality, there are exceptions as to what one *Monkey* could decipher about another. We could apply the same logic to human beings. Of course, applying this modus to understanding every human being might not be that simple.

---

[16] Please keep in mind that I am not comparing human beings with Monkeys in the most fundamental sense.

As already echoed, we are ignorant of our own species. In that sense, there is no way that we could be superior in the wilderness. Hence, we could never be certain of our weakness in the natural milieu.

IGNORANT OF THE SPECIES

While I am a human being, I know little or nothing about my human brethren. There are so many subtle nuances in deciphering the scope of human *Beingness* that it could be impossible to settle a certain reality about the species. I could not speak for the human species, although I could probably speak for myself, at least to some extent.

The proper argument to evoke here is that there is no supreme truth about human beings. All we know is that human beings are indeed in the universe. Whether we are alone in the wilderness is another reality, which very few of us comprehend. We dwell in our ignorance of ourselves. But I am sure that we will one day ascertain whether God or any other living entities, which is (or are) alien to our ways of being, had been watching us from above, from below, from the sidelines, or from within.

The understanding I am endeavoring, so awkwardly I must admit, to convey in this discussion is that, despite the complex nature of human beings, something special sets us apart from the rest of the animal kingdom. The question is what that might be? The answer, as I have sought to articulate throughout this text, is that *we are humans*.

Certainly, we are different from the Chimpanzees, even though we possess a few of its inherent physical traits. We are also distinct from other mammals. Arguably, we are the only sapiens of significance within the natural. Most assuredly, that does not make us supreme in the true sense of the word *Superior*. In saying that, I must admit this conjuncture probably provides us an edge in the natural.

My point is that it is undeniable that human beings enjoy a certain advantage in nature. What we lack in brute physical force, we make up for it in our intellect. We interact with the environment in ways that no other mammals could fathom. Despite our flaws, at times we represent a supreme force in the environment.

We hold talents, we possess skills, which most living entities do not hold or to hold in any respect. We have a sense of self, which strike as being able to surpass that of most living creatures on the planet. But we are hardwired with *Nature*. There is no way out of that reality.

In many respects, we are a genuine beast in nature. We could also act as if the natural had no immediate effects on our beings. We believe that we are wireless beings in nature. I doubt that this is the case in any way, shape, or form. Perhaps, we are a hybrid being in the natural.

At the most intrinsic level, we are different from other wild beasts. Leaving that aside, we are inherently a part of nature itself. For that reason, we could not be as distinct as we would like to be. We could only be as our nature allows us to be. We are only ourselves in the natural.

REASON AND HUMAN SUPREMACY

The argument is that human beings are on top of the food chain. Why would that be the case? Observers have offered several explanations in an attempt to clarify the reason human beings are superior in nature.

One of such explanations is the idea that human beings are the only living entity properly equipped, both physically and mentally, to reason. While I will not challenge this argument here per se, I am not sure this is the case in all instances. Human beings did not invent themselves.

There is more to being than to be able to reason, I am convinced. In saying that, I must point out that for the being to reason, he must be able to communicate with the self. The being must be able to think.

Every living entity can think (and performs this task with ease). We must agree that every living entity could reason. Therefore, human beings could not be superior in nature based on that understanding alone (i.e., based on the human capacity to reason). Without regard to that fact, this understanding does not settle the debate.

We could look at this issue from two angles. On the one hand, we could say that only humans can think. Thus, we are superior to other beings in the natural setting, particularly those that could not perform a similar task. Here, I am referring to living entities that could not think.

From a different angle, we could recognize that every living being could think. In actuality, that does not necessarily mean that they could reason just as human beings perform such a task. The implication here is that thinking is not a human exception. For that reason, human beings could not be superior in nature by virtue of their thinking abilities alone.

It is undeniable that human beings are determined to control their nature. Everything that we do in nature seems designed to allow us to undo our [own] nature. We seem to nourish a burning desire to remove ourselves from the natural. But is that a natural way of being in the nature milieu? I am not sure.

What is unequivocal is that it does not seem as if animals (or other living entities in nature) would like to transcend their *Beingness* from the natural. They do not seem concerned with becoming *super entities* in nature. They do not seem determined to find means, which would allow them to be different from their design.

My point here is that human beings do not seem *willing to be* based on the way nature designed them *to be*. They seem determined to rid themselves of their natural state of being. Human beings seem ill-content with their natural *Beingness*. Of course, we could not say the same for other living beings.

On the face of it all, it could be said that a *Lion* wants to be a *Lion*. A *Dog* enjoys being a *Dog*. A *Cat* seems delighted of being as its nature intended. Yet, when it comes to human beings, the reality is much different.

Human beings strive to be other than their nature intended. We would like to be as ferocious as a *Lion* could be. We would like to be as nimble as a *Cat* could be. We would like to fly like a *Bird*. We would like to run like a *Jaguar*. We would like to swim like a *Fish*. The problem is that we were not designed to be any of that. Yet, in many cases, we have managed to be like many of these animals, at least to some extent.

Why have we been able to be in ways that seem unnatural? Some might say that it is because of our ability to reason. Our capacity to think has catapulted us in the natural in ways that seem unnatural, others would argue.

Without a doubt, human beings stagger along as having an intrinsic introspective insight into their nature. This is the case as opposed to other living entities. Does that raise us to a God-like status in the natural? I am not sure.

NO HUMAN SUPERIORITY

Humanoids have a special way of looking at themselves in the world. We view ourselves as the owners of the world. Does that mean that we a supreme breed of living beings?

Manifestly, we are not superior beings. Yes of course, we come across as if we enjoyed a special place in the natural. We are also able to interact with nature in ways that most living entities could not even fathom. But would that be enough to authenticate our superior state in the world? I am not sure. Perhaps this is not the case at all.

It is unquestionable that, as a species, we enjoy an evolutionary leap in nature. That advantage places us at the crown of the world's affair. Nonetheless, we are still vulnerable in the world.

This is to echo, we are still part of nature. To recap a previous claim, we are wired to the natural. We are still humans. Therefore, we are still subject to the rules and the limits of the *Natural.*

The being should always strive to preserve the self. In order to do so, the being must converse with the self. But the only way to carry out that task is through a thought producing machine. I must point that does not necessarily mean that only human beings are worthy of producing deep thoughts.

You might view the previous statement as a grandiose claim, which I have no means of supporting beyond any doubt. I agree that the preceding viewpoint is bold. Why could it not be the case?

What is there in the natural, which suggests that only humans can think? I am not sure anyone could say with certainty that thinking is only a human reality. We could indulge a bit more in our speculations.

Every living being thinks. Howbeit, what is the extent to which this is true? In the next two chapters, I will explain that this is, as the case might be, the reality for many living entities.

Many of such entities are familiar to the human kind. In short, I will legislate in favor of the notion that human beings are not the sole owner of thought producing. At least, this is not the case in all instances.

9. HUMAN COMMUNICATION

"Ask others for what you truly want but make up for yourself what you truly need." BWJ—June 2014

Something about the human capacity, if not ability, to think seems intrinsic in the species. We could describe human thoughts as a continuity of human language. Thinking is akin to a sublingual conversation the being is having with the self.

There is a link between human thought, human speech, and human language (*see* Figure 9.1). The essence of these faculties still eludes both people who study the human body and those who specialize on the mind. No one knows for certainty what led human being to develop a thought producing tool. Few could clarify the origin of the human thinking as a survival device.

At this point in the debate, we must note that it is still not clear whether a thought is the by-product of a language or whether a language is a display of a thought. What is clear is that a speech could be understood as an expressive statement, which is a derivative of a thought. It is a way to vocalize a thought. We could call this act a tangible idea. It is a way to come about an idea.

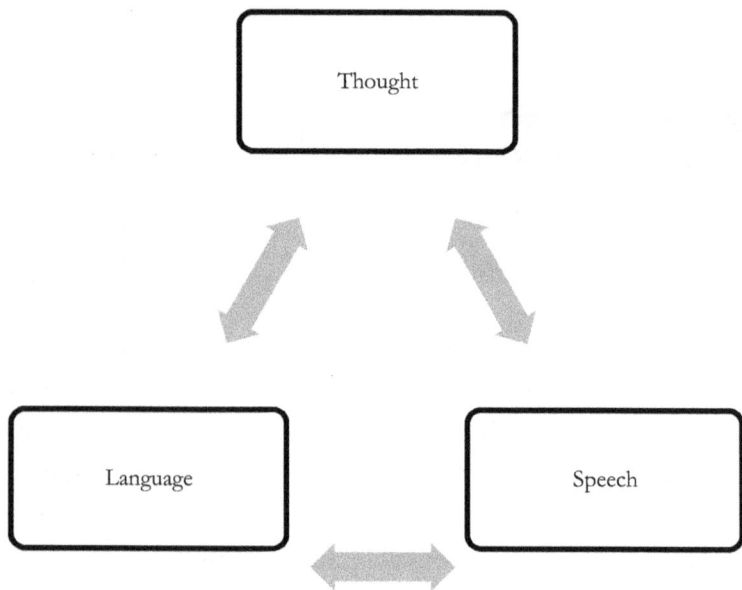

Figure 9.1: The Thought-Producing Process

I would describe the thinking process as the *Chicken* and egg dilemma. It is not settled which came first. The same, it is not clear whether a thought led to language, which, in turn, resulted in speech. For our analysis here, let us say that a co-dependence exists among the three attributes.

Language is a repository of thoughts and ideas, which a person could use to express or to vocalize an idea or a thought. A speech, as a result, is not necessarily an exact representation of the speaker. Rather, a speech is a way for the speaker to express a thought or an idea, which he could do in many different ways.[17]

Two fundamental questions still linger in the debate. First, what makes the speaker express a thought or an idea? Second, where did the thought come from, to begin with? At this point, answers are not definitive.

It is conceivable the being might be projecting a solid state of awareness. But that state could only reveal itself by the mentioned attributions. By the previous understanding, I mean the following: a thought, a language, and a speech.

Human awareness, I subsume, takes many forms. There is not a particular way to be in the world; there is not a specific way to become aware of oneself in the cosmos. Here, we could explain awareness as an acknowledgment of other entities in the natural terrain.

---

[17] There are many ways people could express their selves. They could communicate through body language, sign language, facial expressions, conducts, and display of emotions, just to name a few.

The being might be recognizing a simple fact of seeing something, feeling something, hearing something, or sensing something in the environment.

Suppose you look around. Whatever you see might be interesting to you. As a result, you tell yourself about it. As you communicate with the self about that experience, you become aware of the experience itself. Meanwhile, you are thinking.

Conversation #1

- The being discovers the self
- The being interacts [with Nature]
- Nature interacts with the being

Conversation #2

- The being discovers nature
- The being acknowledges his interaction with nature
- The beingis aware of the interaction between the being and nature
- Nature interacts with the being

Conversation #3

- The being concretizes the interaction with nature
- The being informs the self about the interaction
- The being acknowledges the interaction with nature
- The being concretizes the interaction between the self and nature
- Nature interacts with the being

Figure 9.2: Experiencing the Self

From that logic, we could hypothesize that a thought is a self-induced conversation. That conversation occurs through the following: (a) the place through which the being is interacting with the environment; (b) it takes place while the being admits that correspondence; and (c) it is transcended by telling the self about that connection (*see* Figure 9.2).

A thought is a biological development, which is comprised of various parts. Three important steps are worthy of note in our analysis. The first instrumentation is the back and forth between the world that the individual thinks he is experiencing and the environment that is affecting that world.

The second instrumentation is by recognizing that communication. The final step is to tell the self about that experience (*see* Figure 9.3). The completion of that process concludes with the act of thinking or the act of producing a thought. Above all, a thought allows the being the capacity to discover the self.

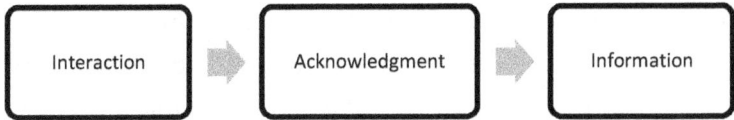

Figure 9.3: Discovering the Self

EVERY LIFE HAS A SOUL

Based on the views echoed thus far, I could say with certainty that every living entity on planet earth could think. The being[18] could not be in the natural setting without enjoying the ability to know that he/it is in the environment. To be is to recognize other beings as either a reflection of the self or something different from the self.

I know I am not a tree when I see a tree standing right before me. I know I am not the river when I see the river streaming in the valley. I know I am not a *Horse* when I see one passing by me. From that knowledge, I

---

[18] In this case, it would not necessarily be a person.

solidify my understanding of my identity in the world. I become certain of my *Beingness* because of other beings.

As I find my way in the natural environment, I might be able to distinguish myself from what I am, what I am supposed to be, what I am not, and what I am not supposed to be. This is the essence of being in nature. This is how I become aware of my environment; this is how I become aware of myself in it. Unless humans are alien beings, this is also how other living beings are aware of themselves in the environment.

Despite making that claim, I would argue the idea that only human beings could think is absurd. If that were to be the case, only humans would settle in the planet. This is to echo, humans would be the only being on earth. Even then, our existence would be precarious; we would be short-lived as a species.

The notion that human beings are superior in nature is an absurdist way of looking at the world. Every being is capable of being aware of the self. When you try to catch a *Chicken*, why do you think the *Chicken* runs away? Why the *Chicken* is seemingly seeking to evade your control of its *Beingness*?

The *Chicken* is always aware of both you and the self (it-self). The *Chicken* also knows that you are seeking to seize its *Beingness*, which means that it might lose that *Beingness*. Thus, the chicken would strive to survive.

Perhaps this is a trivial representation of survival. Even so, it is a relevant way of explaining the notion of survival. Survival is not only a necessity for human beings; it is also an imperative for other living beings. It is so at the most basic level. Every living being must endeavor to stay alive.

What I am saying here is that the *Chicken* would not try to evade just human beings. The *Chicken* would not just seek to prevent human being from seizing it. The *Chicken* would instinctively react in the same manner in the presence of a *Snake*, a *Coyote*, or any other entity that might seek to seize its *Beingness*. The same is true for every living entity in our planet.

The only explanation is that the living entity might see you, hear you, or even sense your presence the same way you might see it, ear it, and feel its presence. The being might convey the gathered information with the self. It might be able to react based on that information.

The being, in this case, the *Chicken*, is aware of the self; it is aware of your presence; it is aware of the environment as well. To that extent, the being is pondering. The being has no alternatives but to ponder. This is the essence of survival.

It could be said that the being is alive. As a result of that state of being, the being has a duty to preserve the self. Omitting other reasons, the being does so at all costs.

The struggle to *live on* in the world is intrinsic in the being's inherent fondness, capacity, or virtue to seize other beings. It is also inherent in the being's capacity to evade other beings; it is natural for the being to avoid becoming the subject of others. This is the essence of the struggle to stay alive. This is the essence of life. Let me expand on that idea a little more.

THE CAPACITY TO BE IN THE WORLD

Nature affords every being the inherent abilities either to seize other beings[19] or to avoid being seized.[20] Every being must be. To that degree, every being has the capacity or the ability to protect the self. Just the same, every being could be seized by other beings.

In the *Chicken* example explained earlier, it is up to you[21] to find a means to outsmart that *Chicken*. It is also up to you to find a way to seize the *Chicken's Beingness*. That skill is important. It is part of a survival mechanism which allows us to preserve our own *Beingness* in the world, at least as a species.

---

[19] By that, I mean offensive mechanisms.

[20] I am also referencing a defensive mechanism.

[21] I am referring to the person who is seeking to appropriate the *Chicken*.

We could all agree that *Chickens* taste wonderful. But aside from the taste, we need that consumption to survive. We do not have any qualms with *Chickens* per se; we just need to survive.

It is up to the *Chicken* to stay out of our way so it might survive. It is also up to us to seek that *Chicken* wherever it might be to prolong our survival. We do so by taming, often feeding, and consuming the *Chicken*.

Our survival depends on the extinction of the *Chicken*. [22] Exclusive of that reality, the death of the *Chicken* is not the end of the *Chicken*.[23] The *Chicken* dies, at least in the flesh, so we live in the soul.

Human beings live on so life continues in nature. We also enjoy a similar affinity with the *Lions*, the *Tigers*, the *Sharks*, and (I would say) any entities that can consume human flesh, except within our own species. Yet, human beings represent a more dangerous reality to themselves or to the human species itself.

The death of a man in the hands of another does not advance the continuity of the human species in the end. Such a conjuncture does not contribute to nature, notably when it comes to its progress in the end. From

---

[22] By that, I mean the individual consumption itself.

[23] I will elaborate on this idea further in a different book project.

then on, there is always a good reason to protect the self, even if we must do so to preserve our own species or to help simplify the continuity of nature.

BEING ABLE TO PHILOSOPHIZE

Every living entity can [and does] think. This is a built-in faculty into the *Beingness* itself, whether a humanoid or else. The being could not be unless it had been aware of the self in the environment.

If *Chickens* were not aware of themselves, they might not have been able to survive long enough to become a relevant entity for our own survival. Could you imagine how easy it would have been to catch a *Chicken* and to consume it at will?[24] The same is true for any other beings in nature, including us.

If we were not aware of ourselves in the environment, we would be vulnerable to every flesh eating entities, even to *Ants* and *Birds*. We would not live long enough to become a primate in the natural. Even so, something else sets us apart from the rest of the animal kingdom. It is irrefutable that we are *Omni potent* and *Omni present* in nature. Therefore, there is more to

---

[24] I am aware of the fact that, in most industrialized countries, many farm *Chickens* in captivity. Still, that does not negate the argument that a *Chicken* has a being just as we humans do.

our *Beingness* than we give ourselves credit, I would further insist.

We do not have to be in the physical nature to experience it. We could imagine being there. We could create the experience of being in the environment.

We could imagine what it would be like to be vulnerable in nature. We could do so by being out there in the world or by imagining ourselves in a particular environment.[25] We often do so based on what others have experienced over time in our world.

The question worth asking here is whether a *Chicken* could communicate with other *Chickens* the same way we are in the habit of doing it with ourselves. The answer is, in all likelihood, no. Only, that does not mean the *Chicken* is helpless in the world. That does not mean that the *Chicken* is without recourse in the universe.

It is proper to say that human beings have a way of starting communications among them. But that way, I would argue, is unique to the species. I would further propose that the *Cows*, the *Monkeys*, the *Chickens*, the *Horses*, the *Dogs*, and the *Cats* of the world have a unique way of communicating among themselves. This is the key to their survival, as the similar trait is the reason of our survival instincts as well.

---

[25] In this case, I am referencing to nature itself.

Since we do not speak *Chicken*, we could not fathom what they are saying as we try to seize them. Again, that does not mean that they do not have a soul just as we do. Despite everything, that does not even mean they do not have the right to be, just as we do. It does not mean the *Chickens* of the world are not survivalists, just as we are or just as we could be.

10. A SURVIVALIST APPROACH

"If your happiness depends on someone else, then you will be unhappy for the rest of your life." BWJ—June 2016

René Descartes claims *"Cogito Ergo Sum,"* which translates, *"I think, therefore I am."* [26] This quote appeared in his famous publication known as the *"Principia Philosophiae,"* which is also known as the *"Principles of Philosophy."* From a Cartesian slant, the understanding is that the act of thinking could lead to many discoveries, one of which is the discovery of the self. From that logic, it could be echoed that thinking is a portal to human introspection.

---

[26] Please see Rene Descartes' popular work on the subject. René Descartes, *Principles of Philosophy: Top Philosophy Collections* (Taniyuki, 2015); René Descartes, *Principia philosophiae* (apud Ludovicum Elzevirium, 1644).

I do not dispute the *Cogito* argument per se. At least, I do not do so based on a rebuttal of the *Cartesian* lens. For all that, I am convinced there is more to [just] *pondering* in the world.

I believe the being must be able to understand the manner of the world itself. The being must grasp the virtue of his *Beingness* in the natural environment. This is the only way for the being to compare his reality and the reality of other beings in the natural setting.

Jean-Paul Sartre further claims, *"Existence Precedes Essence."*[27] In response to that popular understanding, one could argue that existentialism offers little or no road map to the being beyond existing. I would contend that there is more to life than existing and/or pondering.

Life does not stop after existence. Essence does not prolong existence in and of itself, I would further note. I would contend the being must survive beyond his essence. This is indispensable for the being to exist beyond chance.

Existentialism claims that the being is free to be. Except that, I do not see how this is possible, when the

---

[27] This view is a corner stone of existentialism this idea could be found in the works of Jean-Paul Sartre Jean-Paul Sartre, *Existentialism Is a Humanism* (Yale University Press, 2007).and Martin Heidegger Martin Heidegger, *Being and Time: A Translation of Sein Und Zeit* (SUNY Press, 1996).

being is an insignificant part of the environment. The being has no relevance other than the ones granted to him by others.

In a social setting, for instance, the being exists only conjecturally. But in the natural milieu, the being exists conditionally to his wish to survive and his acceptance of his natural state of being. Thus, existence could not precede essence under any circumstance.

The being does not (or could not) define his *Beingness* in the propinquity. Instead, the environment is the one that defines the being. The being is the product of other beings—oftentimes more powerful entities—in the setting where the being lives. Of course, some might argue this is true only within a social context. I could beg to differ.

NO FREEDOM TO BE HAD

The freedom the being supposedly enjoys in his world is often inconsequential to the reality he often finds himself. This is the opposite of the life he lives, which he could not always escape. Sometimes, he has no choice, but to live in this environment, which could be harmful to his *Beingness*. Certainly, the being is free to discover his reality. In all other respects, the being is restricted and/or limited in the way he interacts with that reality.[28]

In the environment, prominently in a social setting, the being could not *be*, unless it received the permission to *be*. Thus, the being is not free to be. The being is only free to accept his conditions.

In like manner, the failure to *be* within the confine of the natural and/or the social milieu could lead to the premature extinction of the being. While the being is never free to be either in nature or in society, he is free to accept his *Beingness*. The being must be against all odds.

In the face of that reality, the being must survive. The being must *be*, even though preserving one's *Beingness* might be impossible or far-fetched. The being must find a way to be against all probable circumstances.

The *"Cogito"* is just the beginning of a lifelong discovery process. The being, in this case a person, only *ponders* so he could prolong his *Beingness*. This is the reason I sought to introduce a distinct intellectual outline in the debate. This is the best way to understand *"Beingness,"* not just that of humans, within the natural environment.

---

[28] The natural environment limits the being, while the social setting restricts the being.

Thus far, I have echoed that my existence, my survival in the world—wherever that world might be—and my *Beingness* are the results of my realization of my presence in my setting. To make my presence real in the environment, I have to be able to reflect introspectively about myself. I have to hold the capacity to reflect on the *Beingness* of other entities in the environment as well.

Because of the previously stated reasons, I note the notion of *"Cogito, Ergo Philosophus."* I would say, *"I think therefore I philosophize."* As a result, the being must be in synchrony with the mundane around him. This is the best way that the being could be beyond a mere existence.

The being must be beyond a mere discovery of the self in the cosmopolitan. The being must do anything or everything to increase his power, his ability, and/or his cleverness to prolong his existence in the grand scheme of the reality he faces. This is important for the being to be.

The being must always philosophize in contemplation of surviving in the world beyond fate or external circumstances. To do so, the being must be practical. The being must understand nature; he must grasp important aspects of the natural. The being must also engage the entities that form the natural. Therefore, the being must always look at the world introspectively.

PROPRIETY ON THOUGHTS

Most observers are of the belief that human beings are the only species on earth that are intellectually competent enough to produce thoughts.[29] It is widely understood that humans are the only animal suitable for reasoning. By now, you would agree this is not necessarily the case.

Based on what I have discussed in this text until that point, I could cast doubt on the notion of human superiority, particularly if it is based on a person's ability

---

[29] Please refer to a piece by Neel Burton regarding seven things that only human beings could do. Neel Burton, "The Seven Things That Only Human Beings Can Do," Psychology Today, accessed January 4, 2018, http://www.psychologytoday.com/blog/hide-and-seek/201208/the-seven-things-only-human-beings-can-do. See another piece by Thomas Suddendorf about what separates humans from other animals. Thomas Suddendorf, "The Science of What Separates Us from Other Animals: Human Imagination and Our Ability to Share Imaginative Scenarios with Others." accessed January 4, 2018, http://www.slate.com/articles/health_and_science/science/2014/03/the_scie nce_of_what_separates_us_from_other_animals_human_imagination_and.ht ml. also see Melissa Hogenboom Melissa Hogenboom, "The Traits That Make Human Beings Unique," accessed January 4, 2018, http://www.bbc.com/future/story/20150706-the-small-list-of-things-that-make-humans-unique. see Charles Q. Choi Charles Q. Choi, Live Science Contributor | March 25, and 2016 01:07pm ET, "Top 10 Things That Make Humans Special," Live Science, accessed January 4, 2018, https://www.livescience.com/15689-evolution-human-special-species.html.

to reason or to think. I am perplexed that thinking is only a human fling. Every living being has the capacity to think; at least, they do so in their own way.

You might evoke the fact that human beings have made certain strives in the natural, which seem to surpass the prowess of any other living entities. Seemingly, human beings are on top of the world. On the face of it all, we seem to dominate the world. We reign over the food chain.

Certain circumstances might explain the reason human beings are on top of the food chain. For example, human beings transfer the impression they enjoy a high ability to produce thoughts, in this instance, deep thoughts. I admit it; this is potentially a huge advantage over the other beings in the wilderness itself.

An alternate argument worth pointing out has a lot to do with the irrefutable fact that there is little evidence to suggest that humans are the only living entities who can think or who can engage in similar roles. There is enough evidence to suggest that thinking is a natural happening. This is a built-in trait in every living entity on the planet. That is why everyone or every living entity in nature does it.

The act of thinking itself is not a universal characteristic in every living being. As mentioned in Chapter 6, there are various degrees of thinking. Some living entities have the leaning to think at a deeper introspective level. Human beings seemingly fall in that category. Nonetheless, a word of caution is worth legislating as we conclude this work.

While I agree that humans could be among the few living beings advanced enough to engage in introspective thinking, I am not sure that they enjoy any propriety on the act of thinking itself. Thinking is a biological attribute of being alive. What that means is that every being that has a brain or other anatomical arrangements similar to a brain for its role could perform the same exercises with ease.

There is no primacy in the art of survival. Every living being must survive. Therefore, every living being must be conscious of their need for survival.

ANY LIVING BEING COULD THINK

Any part of the body, which controls or transfer sensory information from one end of the body to another, could make it possible for the being to engage in a behavior, which would seem similar to the act of thinking. Every animal or every living being could [or must] think. Most living entities have such a purpose. This is the case whether such physiological realms are similar to human beings' anatomical arrangements.

My point is that every being has the faculty to *Cogitate*. This is compulsory (it is almost conditional) for the being to persist in nature. I do not believe that only a specific breed of beings could think. Thus, I do not believe that only human beings could *think*.

What I am saying is that human beings are neither the rule nor the exception, when it comes to thinking. In actuality, I did not delve in this part of the debate. In any event, I am convinced that thinking is not a human affair.

To recap the crux of the argument echoed in this work thus far, let me echo that I was not seeking to examine which entity in nature is qualified for producing thoughts. Rather, the essence of my analysis was to find out the extent of human beings' leaning to produce significant thoughts, which would enable them to prolong their existence both in nature and in other environmental settings, namely a social setting. It was important to make out the extent to which a possible tie exists between human existence and a human ability to philosophize.

As a means to corroborate my argumentations, I referenced that thinking is a natural state of being. I also evoked the possibility that human beings are not the owners of the world, for they are not the only survivors in the world. To make my case, I legislated that every living being must think. Under this rule, I argued that thinking is what affords essence to the living being. As it happens, thinking is also the essence of the *Cogito*.

Chapter 10: A Survivalist Approach

11. THE REALITY OF BEING

"Live your life according to your own reality. Do not be simply for being. Make a difference. Be a survivor." BWJ—June 2017

An important reality about being in the world is worth pointing out in the debate. Not every being is aware of the self in the natural. Not every being understands the need to preserve the self. It could be said that not every being understands the need to make the self a priority in relation to other beings.

This conjuncture often has serious effects on the being. If the being were to become unable *to be*, he might lose his *Beingness* altogether. He might become troubled. He might become dormant (even to the point of death). The being might become the subject of other beings within the environment.

This reality is the essence of the struggle *to be*. No matter what, the being must be. The being must also endeavor to solidify his *Beingness* every moment of his existence. He *must be even* if it is for the sake of being.

Although this understanding might sound simple enough, it could be hard to explicate in practical terms. The reality of every being is different. As a result, most beings forgo their *Beingness.* Some do so consciously. Others are induced to do so. This might explain the reason that, within the human species itself, some beings are preys, while others are predators or even both (at times).

EXISTENCE AND BEING

Existence is a part of being. It is not being per se. For instance, in order to be, the being must find a way to maintain his existence. Without considering other hindrances, finding a means to subsist is not always possible.

An existence must be maintained at all costs. Otherwise, it runs the risks of becoming the nothingness. Let us consider a few important issues.

Maintaining one's existence, for instance, often requires the destructions of other beings in one's milieu. This is the essence of being in the natural. In any case, the being could only be by preventing other beings from being.

The being does not automatically become aware that he is condemned to be or not to be at his own discretion. The being does not always grasp that he must strive to find the means to survive outside the desires of others. Under a similar circumstance, the being might give up on the self.

What makes the being be? The being could arrive at the conclusion that he needs to be by realizing that he must survive. To do so, the being must engage in deep thinking; the being must engage in introspection. The being must cogitate. Thus, the *Cogito* is the core of the *Beingness*.

I described the *Cogito* as a self-scrutiny. Under such an instance, the being is engaged in the act of thinking. In this case, thinking could be defined as an infinite conversation. The being is entertaining the conversation with the self. Only, he is doing so introspectively, at times even unconsciously.

As the being engages the environment, he examines the self in that milieu. He does so based on the reality he is experiencing at any given point. As the being converses with the self, he is informing the self about the self. He is informing the self about the milieu where the self finds itself.

Informing the self about the self in the environment is what I described as the act of thinking. The being is able to gauge the self. The being is able to gauge the environment. The being is able to gauge the self in the environment.

The ability to think, as I articulated in this book, is the essence of the *Cogito*. When the being ponders, he is in synchrony with nature. He is in synchrony with the world itself. While the being engages both himself and the world around him, he learns to value that reality.

As the being becomes familiar with the act of *Cogitating*, he becomes harmonious with both the self and the world around the self. This is the crux of the *"Cogito."* In saying that, I reckon that the nature of the being is more complex than that. In any case, I offered a routine audit to grasp the nature of human beings.

I admit that there is more to humanness than a mere acknowledgment of existence. I also understand that the debate can be inconsistent on this issue. I sought to change that reality however so slightly in this work. In spite of the contentious nature of the discourse, I hope this book was able to make a tangible difference in the debate.

A NARROW APPROACH

I did not explore the term philosophy in a surgical sense in this manuscript.[30] I did not assess the extent to which other species have the means, be it physical, mental, or else, to engage in introspective thinking. The focus of this book was to examine the degree to which philosophy could help human beings lengthen their existence in their world.

The questions I posed here had more to do with the degree to which being able to *ponder* could help the being survive even when he might be deprived of the means of survival? The only way to examine this question is by assessing the being from a practical lens. But we must explore the tribe of the being in a context-specific setting.

We must examine the being not only in a natural context, but we must also do so based on a social lens. We must explore the extent to which human existence depends on the beings' preference to *ponder* at an introspective level. There is only one way to be. That way, I am convinced, is to be in synchrony with the world.

---

[30] See the text titled *We Have No Clue.*

The being must become aware of the self to be on the same plane field with the environment. Even though that conjuncture might only be possible through introspection, the being must strive to achieve that feat. The being must be at all costs and under any circumstance.

Yes, I offered a narrow approach to understand the human reality. I also asserted that there is always a need for the being to preserve his *Beingness*. Nonetheless, I would argue that self-preservation is not a given. The being does not always have the luxury to preserve the self.

BEING RESPONSIBLE FOR THE SELF

In the book titled *Men and Racism*, I argued that the being does not have an inherent responsibility to be in the world. The being could not be a certain way. I argued that nature supersedes the being in all instances. Likewise, society supersedes the being in every imaginable way.

I explained the role of nature in stirring the being in the right direction, which is not necessarily the right direction for the being himself. Rather, nature tends to stir the being in the right direction for the benefits of the natural. There is no doubt that the being has the final responsibility of protecting the self. The problem is the being (or the humanoid) seldom does so measurably and/or efficiently.

What I mean by the previous statements is that the being enjoys a more marked ability and/or the competence to assess his *Beingness* in the earthly reality where he lives. This is why, I also argue, it is up to the being to preserve the self. The being must find his (own) way to be in both the natural haunt and the artificial (social) environment. In saying that, I am not making the irreconcilable argument that the being is free to be.

I do not challenge the existentialist argument in itself. I do not argue the being is free to further his *Beingness* without natural obstacles or any artificial hindrance. Anyhow, the view I was trying to get across is the notion the humanoid (or the being) enjoys an intrinsic ability and/or an inherent fondness to strengthen his survival in the landscape by learning about the pad.

In whatever way, the being must survive by understanding and anticipating the natural and the artificial. He must explore the entities that constitute that setting. From here, the being must *ponder*. This is the only way for the being *to be* beyond chance. This is the only way for the being *to be* not because of serendipity.

I hope that I have been able to echo that connection as convincingly as possible here. I also hope you have found this reading exercise rewarding. In any case, I hope that I have been able to explain to you— in a concise manner of course—the need to think or to ponder.

FINAL THOUGHTS

CONCLUSION AND MISCELLANEOUS

CONCLUSION

"Live your life as it was meant to be lived. There is only one time to live your life; it is right now." BWJ—June 2016

I collated this short paperback under the understanding that philosophizing is an integral part of being. Throughout this work, I contended that the being[31] must philosophize. This is the only means for the being to counterbalance the grip of *Mother Nature*, I echoed.

I also sought to explain the goal of every being is to lengthen his *Beingness* where he/she or it lives. As you might imagine, the challenge was to provide enough proof to support that argument beyond any doubt.

---

[31] In this instance, I am referring to a person.

Whether I succeeded in this strive remains an open-ended question, which the reader (you of course) would have to answer or contemplate at some point.

Keep in mind that this work is mostly the result of speculations. The text is not based on a study or any empirical investigation. In such a manner, the arguments featured here only reflect my unbridled opinion about the subject. You could either accept it or you might challenge it. Of course, I would prefer the former rather than the latter.

LET US PHILOSOPHIZE

Let me echo that I do not engage any third party (individuals) or any other entities in the views expressed here. I must also confide that I developed the positions I explained in this manuscript as an intellectual means to incite a vivid discussion about the subject. I encourage you (i.e., the reader) to remain open-minded and intellectually receptive, even after you finished reading the manuscript.

My central thesis rests on the viewpoint that the being must find a way to preserve his *Beingness* in the face of imminent extinction. This is the essence of human existence in the world. To fulfill that need, the being must be in constant communication with nature. Therefore, the being must philosophize.

Instead of a conclusion, let me say that the quintessence of this work centered on the notion that the ability to think is an important component of finding the necessary means to prolong one's existence and, by extension, the human existence as a whole. Human existence, I argued here, is conditional on the being's own quality to think and to communicate with nature. I also argued that every living entity can and does think. Put differently, human beings are not the exception to that reality, although we are not the rule either.

RECONSIDERING OURSELVES

Human beings have done spectacular things in the natural milieu. We have been to the moon. We have created gadgets, which orbit around the planet. We have created tools and instruments, which have penetrated the universe in ways that few living entities on the planet are aware. We have been able to tap into nature in ways that even ourselves have yet to understand. We are at the vanguard of our planet's evolution in the cosmos. We have done, we have been, and we still on the verge. As a species, we have surpassed our own expectations.

Despite our skills or the potential thereof, we have not carried out anything tangible outside our abilities. The argument could be made that we have not done anything we could not do or anything we were not supposed to do. To that extent, we are not a rare breed of living beings. We are still anchored in nature. We are still the objects of our nature.

Everything human beings have done has only been relevant to the species itself. We have not discovered anything about the world, which would have no effect on us. Even our most prized possessions, including splitting the atom, is only consequential to our own *Beingness*. Despite all of our accomplishments, we are still subject to nature. We are still wired to *Mother Nature*.

This brings us to a few interesting questions, many of which have been asked, explored, and debated extensively in the literature. They include the following: Who are we? Why are we here? What is our purpose? How far would we get as a species? What would become of us if we were to find out that we are not alone in the universe? What would become of our beliefs or values if we were to find out that God has never been alive? What would we do to reconcile our past with our present? How would we carry on if we were to find out the virtue we had been seeking all along has always been within reach? How would we settle the fact that there is only one life to live?

I am not sure how to answer these questions. I am not sure anyone could try to answer them. Aside from that reality, I would say that the mere fact we could consider such predicaments should be enough reasons to make us reconsider our *Beingness* in the world today.

This is the best way to be beyond chance. This is the essence of self-introspection. This is the essence of self-preservation. This is the essence of the *Cogito*. So, let us *think*; let us *philosophize* or should I say: let us *cogitate*.

Conclusion

BIBLIOGRAPHY

Burton, Neel. "The Seven Things That Only Human Beings Can Do." Psychology Today. Accessed January 4, 2018. http://www.psychologytoday.com/blog/hide-and-seek/201208/the-seven-things-only-human-beings-can-do.

Choi, Charles Q., Live Science Contributor | March 25, and 2016 01:07pm ET. "Top 10 Things That Make Humans Special." Live Science. Accessed January 4, 2018. https://www.livescience.com/15689-evolution-human-special-species.html.

Descartes, René. *Principia philosophiae.* Apud Ludovicum Elzevirium, 1644.

———. *Principles of Philosophy: Top Philosophy Collections.* Taniyuki, 2015.

Harper, Douglas. "Online Etymology Dictionary," 2017 2001.

http://www.etymonline.com/index.php?term=phil osophy.

Heidegger, Martin. *Being and Time: A Translation of Sein Und Zeit.* SUNY Press, 1996.

———. *Being and Time: A Translation of Sein Und Zeit.* SUNY Press, 1996.

Hogenboom, Melissa. "The Traits That Make Human Beings Unique." Accessed January 4, 2018. http://www.bbc.com/future/story/20150706-the-small-list-of-things-that-make-humans-unique.

Oxford, Reference. "Fight-or-Flight Response - Oxford Reference." Accessed January 4, 2018. http://www.oxfordreference.com/view/10.1093/oi/authority.20110803095817447.

Sartre, Jean-Paul. *Existentialism Is a Humanism.* Yale University Press, 2007.

Suddendorf, Thomas. "The Science of What Separates Us from Other Animals: Human Imagination and Our Ability to Share Imaginative Scenarios with Others." Accessed January 4, 2018. http://www.slate.com/articles/health_and_science/science/2014/03/the_science_of_what_separates_us_from_other_animals_human_imagination_and.html.

INDEX

BELOW IS A LIST [index] of words and other popular phrases, which had been echoed throughout the manuscript. Bear in mind this list is not exhaustive. Also, be aware that the eBook version of this text does not include an index.

Index

Index

Index

Index

Index

ABOUT THE AUTHOR

BEN WOOD JOHNSON, Ph.D.

 Dr. Ben Wood Johnson is a social observer. He is a multidisciplinary scholar. He writes about Philosophy, Legal Theory, and Foreign Policy. He also writes about Education (School Leadership), Politics, Ethics, Race, and Crime.

Dr. Johnson is a Penn State graduate. He holds a Doctorate in Educational Administration/Leadership, a Master's degree in Political Science, a Master's degree in Public Administration, and a Bachelor's degree in Criminal Justice.

Dr. Johnson worked in law enforcement. He attended John Jay College of Criminal Justice. He is fluent in many languages, including, but not limited to, English, French, Spanish, Portuguese, and Italian.

Dr. Johnson enjoys reading, poetry, painting, and music. You may contact Dr. Johnson by using the information listed below.

OTHER INFO

If you would like to contact Dr. Ben wood Johnson, you may do so by referring to the information listed below.

Mailing/Postal Info:
Eduka Solutions
330 W. Main St #214
Middletown, PA 17057

Electronic Address:

E-mail Address: benwoodpost@gmail.com

Other Info:

Find the author (Ben Wood Johnson) on the following media platforms.

Official Twitter handle: @benwoodpost

Official Facebook Page: @benwoodpost

Official blog (Ben Wood Post) at:
www.benwoodpost.com

Official website: www.drbenwoodjohnson.com

Official academic website at:
www.benwoodjohnson.com

You may also sign up to receive regular updates about Dr. Johnson's activities.

OTHER WORKS

Other works by Dr. Ben Wood Johnson include the following:

1. Racism: What is it?

2. Sartrean Ethics: A Defense of Jean-Paul Sartre as a Moral Philosopher

3. Jean-Paul Sartre and Morality: A Legacy Under Attack

4. Sartre Lives On

5. Forced Out of Vietnam: A Policy Analysis of the Fall of Saigon

6. Natural Law: Morality and Obedience

7. Le Racisme et le Socialisme: La Discrimination Raciale dans un Milieu Capitaliste

8. International Law: The Rise of Russia as a Global Threat

9. Être Noir: Quel Malheur!

10. L'homme et le Racisme: Être Responsable de vos Actions et Omissions

11. Pennsylvania Inspired Leadership : A Roadmap for American Educators

12. Adult Education in America: A Policy Assessment of Adult Learning

13. Striving to Survive: The Human Migration Story

14. Adult Education in America

15. Pennsylvania Inspired Leadership

www.ingramcontent.com/pod-product-compliance
Lightning Source LLC
Chambersburg PA
CBHW021144090426
42740CB00008B/938